3 1336 00327 7077

D0053849

THE SUGAR PILL

An Essay on Newspapers

by

T. S. MATTHEWS

SIMON AND SCHUSTER · NEW YORK

PUBLISHED BY SIMON AND SCHUSTER, INC.
ROCKEFELLER CENTER, 630 FIFTH AVENUE
NEW YORK 20, N. Y.

FIRST PRINTING

LIBRARY OF CONGRESS CATALOG CARD NO.: 59-6008
MANUFACTURED IN THE UNITED STATES OF AMERICA
PRINTED BY THE MURRAY PRINTING COMPANY, FORGE VILLAGE, MASS.
BOUND BY AMERICAN BOOK—STRATFORD PRESS, INC., NEW YORK

To Martha, without whom . . .

CONTENTS

FOREWORD

This is a book with a thesis. It is not a thesis that can be proved, but perhaps a case can be made for it. The thesis is that the Press is not our daily bread but our daily sugar pill. I should be the first to admit that the pill is habit-forming. Whether it is also harmless is another question.

Of the thousands of different brands on the market I have chosen to consider two: one the *Daily Mirror*, because it is the biggest seller in the world; and the other the *Manchester Guardian*, because I like its flavour.

PART I

Journalism

THE FIRST THING in any discussion is to get it clear just what you're discussing. What do I mean by "journalism"? Matthew Arnold called it "literature in a hurry". I certainly don't mean that; it's much too vague—and condescendingly literary. Perhaps you can draw a line between literature and journalism. I can only say that there's a difference which is sometimes easy to see and sometimes not: they overlap and blur into each other. The best journalism approaches literature, and sometimes gets there; and many books are obviously journalism. The speeches of U.S. Presidents are not usually classed as literature, and in fact have often been written by professional journalists. But don't forget the Gettysburg Address. And Somerset Maugham, who ought to know, says that the average life of a novel is 90 days. Journalism tries to communicate facts and information to as many people as possible, while literature tries to express a personal view of life to one person at a time. That may be true but it's not very helpful. There's a line to be drawn somewhere, but smudgily, with a rule of thumb.

And what about the radio, the cinema, television, advertising? If journalism is mass communication, surely they should be included. Hollywood delivers its message in countries where the *Times* never penetrates. When Robert Hutchins and twelve other distinguished Americans made a report in 1947 on *A Free and Responsible Press*, they did include all the "mass media" of communication. As a result, the report, which tried to take in too much, was too abstract, and the Press, which had thought it was sitting for its portrait, was disappointed or annoyed.

Two years later appeared a British report on the Press. This one was more official, the work of a Royal Commission appointed by Parliament to investigate charges that a handful of Press Lords were getting a monopoly of Britain's newspapers. Besides being very much longer than the Hutchins report, it was much more detailed and concrete, and less ambitious. In order to investigate the charge of monopoly the Commission decided to find out all it could about newspapers—who owned them, how an issue was put together, what newspapermen thought they were doing, etc., etc. The Commission made a thorough job of it, and by the time it had reached the conclusion that the charge of monopoly was unfounded it had incidentally drawn a life-size and recognisable portrait of the British Press.

The Hutchins report seems to me typically American: ambitious, high-principled, abstract; and the Royal Commission's characteristically British: cautious, common-sensible and down to cases. To include all forms of mass communication under journalism is a logical but unwieldy idea. Journalism in effect is the Press, and the Press in effect is newspapers.[1]

Newspapers differ from one another almost as widely as a television commercial from a broadcast symphony. They also differ in much the same way as people do, and most newspapers have distinct personalities. When a new paper is "born", the chief care of the men who conceived it is to develop its personality and make it popular or otherwise successful—and once they've developed the paper's personality, to keep it going. Though newspapers consciously try to be different and pride themselves on their difference, they are also extremely insistent that they are members of the same Press. But "the Press", like "the Church", does not really exist except as a diverse collection of schismatic and warring units which regard one another with varying degrees of hostility as blasphemers, heretics, Pharisees and those who have sold their soul to the devil for a price. Oddly enough, this doesn't prevent the Press from thinking of itself as an entity, particularly when some of its members feel that their privileges or perquisites are threatened. On these occasions the Press does show a certain solidarity.

[1] This takes in daily and weekly newspapers, and weekly journals which comment on the news.

But it's only a show: even when the ranks are closed a conscious difference divides the Press into two camps.

Such earnest undertakings as the *Times* of London, the *Times* of New York, the *Manchester Guardian*, the St. Louis *Post-Dispatch*, the London *Daily Telegraph*—in England they call themselves "the quality Press"—are dedicated to enlightening the public. Then there are papers like the New York *Daily News*, the London *Daily Express*, *Sketch* and *Daily Mirror*, and the Hearst Press. They call themselves "the popular Press", which is a more up-to-date term than the old "yellow Press". The relation of these papers to the public is less clear: their purpose seems to be to excite rather than enlighten. And then there are the hundreds of other papers with a foot in both camps.

The curious thing is that, although these two groups, the "quality" and the "popular" papers, pretend they aren't competing, both claim to be the "real" Press and stubbornly insist that the other is a faker. The quality papers, and their adherents, say that the Press should be judged and is truly represented only by the performance and intentions of the better newspapers. To which the mass-circulation papers reply that the vast majority of the public is on their side. In any realistic sense, say the popular papers, we *are* the Press. If you want to see what the Press really is and does, you can't afford to rule out nine-tenths of it. In a democracy shouldn't the majority prevail?

These two extreme wings of journalism do not always despise one another as much as they say they do in public. The popular Press can afford to temper its contempt with kindliness, while the quality Press can't help feeling some alarm. For the fact is that they are in competition, and the prize is survival. Meantime both sides keep up the fiction that the other side is of no importance and that they are both on the same side, really. Thanks to this pretence the Press is still able to think of itself as the Press. As such, it makes certain claims for itself which at this point we might consider.

first and perhaps the greatest claim that the Press makes f, or that is made for it, is that it gives a true report of going on in the world. Is that claim justified?

The report it does print is published quickly and sold cheap. As the Royal Commission admiringly noted: "A newspaper is one of the most remarkable products of modern society. To gather news from five continents; to print and distribute it so fast that what happens at dawn in India may be read before breakfast in England; to perform the feat afresh every twenty-four hours; and to sell the product for less than the price of a box of matches—this, were it not so familiar, would be recognised as an astonishing achievement."

But no newspaper claims that its report contains all the news there is. The New York *Times's* slogan—"All the news that's fit to print"—admits that the *Times* is not telling all it knows. What nearly every newspaper does claim is this: that it prints a fair and significant sample, the pick of the day's news. That sample is chosen, arranged and presented to fit the interests and suit the prejudices of the paper's readers. Another way of saying it: to match the paper's personality. The editors of the paper share the same interests and prejudices, or have adopted them for professional reasons. Though "quality" papers like the *Times* of New York and the *Times* of London can be counted on to report, at length, news of far-away events, the bulk of the news in both papers is "domestic". And the popular Press in each country is as local as the parish pump: it mainly ignores "foreign" news or gives it a lick and a promise (unless it is obviously sensational or can be made to seem so) and concentrates on "news" that comes closer home to its readers' business and bosoms.

From the gigantic dump heap piled up daily by reporters and news services, the Press picks and chooses what to report. How trustworthy is the news it does print? The public's attitude towards this question is a queer mixture of gullibility and scepticism. People are usually, but not always, sceptical about papers they do not like and therefore don't read. The reason "you can't believe what you read in the papers", they say, is because crooked or cynical reporters, either on their own hook or on orders from some higher-up, deliberately misrepresent, invent or suppress the facts. Or, if the reporter is not to blame, his copy is warped, cut or slanted in the office to suit the policy of the paper or the apoplectic temper of the owner.

But it doesn't work quite that way. Crooked reporters don't last long in their jobs, wicked sub-editors are even more prone to ulcers and alcoholism than the righteous, and proprietors, even though some of them want to be and sometimes imagine that they are absolute tyrants, in fact haven't got that much control. But, to judge by the results, it *might* work like that. It's true that Press reports are not always completely accurate, and that comparatively accurate reports are sometimes edited, headlined or cut into versions that misrepresent the original. John Gordon, editor of the London *Sunday Express*, once sent a memo to his staff in which he said: "I do not wish to be hypercritical, but the plain fact is—and we all know it to be true—that whenever we see a story in a newspaper concerning something we know about, it is more often wrong than right." The Royal Commission on the Press, which quoted him, commented: "This is a striking and perhaps, if applied to the newspaper Press as a whole, an extreme statement; but in our experience it has a substantial element of truth."

Then there's the tricky business of emphasis. In the words of the Royal Commission:

> By constantly selecting items of news which supported its own policy and omitting others, or by giving more prominence to events and aspects of affairs having this tendency than to others, a newspaper could in an extreme case produce in the minds of its readers an impression totally divorced from the truth. And it could do this while preserving the most meticulous accuracy in its statement of the facts reported. Political bias may also find expression in the misstatement of facts or their statement in a manner designed

to produce a particular effect on the reader's mind. Factual reports may be interlarded with comment, or comment may be implied in the reports themselves by the use of words carrying overtones of approbation or disparagement.

The sceptical reader does right to be sceptical of the Press's infallibility: but he does wrong in too freely attributing the Press's failures to tell the whole truth and nothing but the truth to the venality of reporters or the rascality of editors. There is a much less dramatic and more reasonable explanation: pressure of time, number of hands engaged—and the nature of the job.

In the collection of news from a number of sources of varying trustworthiness, its transmission by cable, telephone or teleprinter, its sub-editing and its translation into type, the opportunities for error are enormous. They are increased by the speed at which the work must be done and the number of people who have a share in doing it.

A daily newspaper can seldom be certain of its facts in the sense, for example, in which a nautical almanac is certain of its facts. Facts which are not beyond dispute are often news, and news is too ephemeral to acquire the authenticity conferred by investigation and proof. A daily newspaper is obliged by the character of its material to treat as ascertained facts pieces of information of widely differing reliability. Much of its information is obtained by one fallible human being from another, usually by word of mouth. If the informant himself is reliable, he may be misunderstood by a journalist unfamiliar with his technicalities or with points which to the expert are too obvious to mention; if the informant is not certain of his facts, he may mislead the journalist. Even an eyewitness's account may be untrustworthy, particularly if the witness is a member of the public not trained to observe accurately and tells his story in an atmosphere of excitement. Not all news reports come from one person or from people in a position to know the truth, and when the sources are many and indirect the risks of inaccuracy are multiplied. . . .

Journalists naturally try to make a good story, to find an interesting angle, to devise a headline to catch the reader's attention, to miss nothing that a competitor has found and yet if possible to be different and more original. The art of journalism consists in doing all these things, and up to a point it is valuable that they should be done, because by them readers are encouraged to read important news which otherwise would not interest them. But there are obvious dangers in pushing too far the effort to attract.

Newspapers often suppress news. Sometimes they do it from patriotic motives, as in the British Press's conspiracy of silence about Edward VIII and Mrs. Simpson. But every day, in the ordinary course of events, papers suppress news constantly and more or less consistently: some because it's indecent—though their opinions on what constitutes indecency vary a great deal —some because it's libellous, but most because it's not "their kind of news". The New York *Daily News's* meat is the New York *Times's* poison, and vice versa.

I made an itemised list of the contents of two newspapers (the London *Daily Mirror* and the *Manchester Guardian*) for the same day. The *Mirror* is a tabloid whose pages are less than half the size of the *Guardian's*. Though that day's issue contained 20 pages to the *Guardian's* 14, the *Mirror's* headlines, features and lay-outs take up so much of its space that comparatively little is left for straight news. Of the 144 news stories[1] which the two papers printed between them, 9 were reported by both, 23 by the *Mirror* only, and 71 by the *Guardian* only. Some minor news items in each paper were sent in by special correspondents, and so might be regarded as not available to both papers, but in general both the *Mirror* and the *Guardian* were reporting the supposedly newsworthy events of the same day. The key to

[1] Not including sports and some business "stories" which are mostly impossible to classify as strictly news, or are printed in tabular form, etc.

their striking difference is the word "newsworthy". The *Mirror* that day suppressed scores of news stories which it considered not worth reporting to its enormous audience in its limited space. And the *Guardian* suppressed nearly a dozen news items that appeared in the *Mirror* for the same reason: it wasn't interested.

This brings up the question: don't newspapers know what news is? But of course they do—news is what's newsworthy, and what's newsworthy depends on who's talking. By "newsworthy" the *Mirror* means one thing and the *Guardian* another; and so on up and down the line. They really mean "*Mirror*-worthy", "*Guardian*-worthy", etc.

Then what becomes of the Press's claim that it gives a true report of what's going on in the world? How can it claim to do that, when its report varies so widely, and so subjectively, from paper to paper? The Press's defence is various, vigorous, contradictory and unconvincing. Some assert that it's wrong to be impartial, impossible to be objective. Others (e.g., the New York *Times*) insist that the Press (or the *Times*, at least) is in fact objective, within the limits of decency, and can be trusted to report truthfully and as fully as necessary on everything that is needful to know. The *Times* implies that most other papers, unfortunately, cannot be so trusted. The tabloid Press sneers at this attitude, which it calls hypocritical and pompous. What on earth is the use, it says, of printing masses of stuff "for the record" which no one will read? The first duty of a paper is to get itself read; so pick the news that will attract the attention and hold the interest of most readers, and let the rest go, it will never be missed.

All papers exercise choice in what news to report and what to suppress, and this choice is necessarily subjective. The editors who choose the news are not following their noses; they are veteran professionals, guided by the rules of their trade and the tradition of their paper—but they are following the paper's nose. As a personality their paper is interested in certain news items and not interested in others. What this amounts to is that the Press doesn't agree on what news is. It also doesn't agree on how to report it.

The news is first picked to suit the personality of the paper and then written to suit it. At one extreme it's written in a colourless, factual, ploddingly detailed account; at the other extreme in a colourful, lively, condensed narrative—an attempt to tell the facts as a "story". The one may be as dry as an official bulletin, the other as garish as a comic strip; both claim to tell the same piece of news. One tries to keep bare facts in perfect balance, the other to sketch a perfect likeness in three quick lines and a blob of colour. Between these two extremes of the factual report (in which some facts may be wrong or missing, or the emphasis slightly or altogether askew) and the colourful story (in which facts may be condensed or subordinated to "the story line" in order to make a stab at the truth) lies a gamut of reporting techniques that are liable to share the errors of both extremes.

Picking the news and telling it are both done to suit a paper's personality. Another way of saying it is that all newspapers are biased. Most people regard most of the Press as biased, but not the paper they read, whose bias they happen to share. The Press itself holds this view, perhaps to a greater extent than the public; every paper knows exactly what the bias of its fellows is, on almost every subject. It may even admit to a certain bias itself. Nevertheless, this question of bias causes continual uneasiness within the Press. The uneasiness, I think, has something to do with the relation between the paper's personality and the mainly anonymous journalists who serve it. In earlier days all journalists were anonymous, but today, although a few old-guard papers still keep to the tradition, most of the Press give "by-lines" to their star reporters and feature-writers. Some compromise by allowing pseudonyms (e.g., "Cassandra" or "Our Washington Correspondent") and by attributing despatches to the Press service that sent them in. In so far as a paper permits the intrusion of other personalities it endangers its own: that's the gist of the argument for anonymity and against signed journalism. Anonymity enhances the paper's personality; the anonymous voices combine into one voice, the paper's.

The personality of a paper is its most valued and most jealously guarded possession. It is

> compounded not merely of its physical appearance and its political policy, but also of its tone and style, its unspoken assumptions and its subtle relationship with its readers. This personality is its greatest asset: it is the deposit of years; and it can be destroyed almost overnight. The necessity of preserving it imposes on those who control the paper a limitation less obvious than those of time, space and cost. A newspaper can act as the vehicle of another personality, whether that of editor or proprietor, only within the limits set by its own. It cannot radically alter its character without destroying itself. . . .

The Press feels the difficulty in reconciling these facts: that a personality must have bias, to a greater or less degree; that a paper must preserve its personality; that most papers would prefer to be considered as unbiased, because the Press claims to give a true report of what's going on in the world, and a biased report cannot be a true report. Some papers try to wriggle off the horns of this dilemma by denying bias in their own case, no matter how frequently they recognise it in others. An amusing example was given by *Time* in its early days, when it announced that its view of the world would be that of "the man in the moon, at the close of the current century". *Time* has since come down to earth.

Thanks to the tremendous increase in news-gathering services and in the speed of transmitting news, the Press is already swamped under more news than it can handle. There's too much of it to be taken in by one paper's personality. Yet there are still large areas of the world from which no news comes, just as there are large sections of the world's population to which no news goes—in the form of newspapers, at least. The Press cannot report all the news. And the news it does report is liable to inaccuracies, mistakes and omissions of fact, misplacements of emphasis.

In short, to get a true report of what's going on in the world, even the Western world, you'd have to read quite a lot o different newspapers and try to piece them together. And even then the fragments wouldn't always fit. The Press's answer to this is: No; fragments will do; no one ever really gets more than that; and if you want the biggest or truest fragments, read *our* paper.

Another claim the Press makes is that it has been given a charter to inform and admonish the public. That's the assumption the Press operates on, anyway. But who conferred this charter? In so far as it exists, the public conferred it. Certain papers by a long record of excellence have achieved a position of public trust; and it is almost as if those papers had really been given such a charter. But in fact that charter was self-conferred in each case when the paper first started publication and announced, modestly or otherwise, its intention to inform its readers and admonish them when they needed admonishing. After long years, sometimes generations, of building up the paper's reputation as a trustworthy informant and admonisher, the charter it conferred on itself has been as it were countersigned by the public. So runs the argument of the "quality Press". The "popular Press" now claims its right to the same charter and flaunts the countersign of a much larger public. As long as it has the big battalions of readers on its side, the popular Press can make any claims it feels like making, and get away with them. Its argument is that its charter has been conferred by divine right—the divine right of the people. Dean Inge's famous remark that "democracy is the divine right of kings standing on its head" would never be applauded by the popular Press.

The Press as a whole knows, it's true, that the continuance of this unwritten charter depends finally on the continued favour of the public. The popular Press sees the whole thing quite simply in terms of circulation. If you peddle enough papers you can admonish the public to beat hell, and give an impression, at least, of getting results too. The quality Press knows it has to hang on to enough readers to keep in business, but it really does believe in operating under a charter, and feels the eyes of the great dead looking over its shoulder. The popular Press finds this funny, or pathetic.

Another claim that is sometimes made for the Press is that it speaks for the nation. On rare occasions, yes; when there is a national consensus of feeling (e.g., in the U.S. just after the Japanese attack at Pearl Harbor, or in Britain when she went to war in 1939). And when the nation is uncertain or arguing with itself, the uncertainty or the argument is echoed by the Press's many and contradictory tongues. But ordinarily the Press is a Babel, not a Pentecost. After the fact, one part of the Press or even one paper may claim to have spoken for the nation —if the majority faction is indeed the nation. After the British General Election of 1945 it was the *Daily Mirror*, not the London *Times*, that could say "I told you so!" But there have been some embarrassing slip-ups: in the U.S. Presidential Election of 1948 most of the U.S. Press predicted a landslide for Dewey, and the landslide went the other way. And in the 20 years of Democratic government the overwhelming majority of the U.S. Press were the mouthpieces of Republican publishers, while the nation silently and persistently voted against its "voice".

An even shakier claim is that the Press is the principal means of communication between nations. In the English-speaking Press foreign news is reported either by correspondents (who don't always know what they're talking about) or by translated gobbets from the foreign Press. In the popular Press, which is the only reading of the vast majority of Americans and British, foreign despatches of any sort are few and far between. Many more people in both countries, and even more in the rest of the world, get their "news" and impressions of America and Britain from the cinema. Here America has much the bigger circulation but Britain gets the "better Press".

The Hutchins Commission believed "that if people are exposed to the inner truth of the life of a particular group, they will gradually build up respect for and understanding of it." Americans are indignant or dismayed because of the "misunderstanding" of the U.S. and the disrespect for its way of life which U.S. movies have spread throughout the world. It must be that Hollywood has misinterpreted or failed to interpret the inner truth of American life. Some Americans feel this so strongly that they want certain U.S. films censored or suppressed.

The Press claims to be the necessary daily bread of the people—in a democracy, at least. Here again it doesn't so much claim this as assume it, and almost everybody accepts this assumption as true. The Hutchins Commission stated it as a self-evident fact: "The Press has become a vital necessity in the transaction of the public business of a continental area . . . essential to the operation of the economy and to the government of the Republic." Advertising men make almost the same claim for the "economic necessity" of advertising. But don't forget that when the Hutchins Commission says "the Press" it means all the kinds of mass communication there are. And we're talking about newspapers.

Are newspapers really necessary? When a strike shuts down newspapers over a whole region, the public may be annoyed, but life seems to go on pretty much as usual. Radio can and does broadcast "essential" information, and spreads it wider and faster than newspapers can. Rebecca West says, "A community must have news, as it must have fuel, food, and clothing. It needs news for the same reason that a man needs eyes. It too has to see where it is going." That's what the circulation-promotion managers claim, too. In Russia, with a controlled Press, they don't need circulation-promotion managers; the Russian Press has a monopoly on supplying the demand of the community to "see where it is going". But the helter-skelter of news in our free Press and its contradictory interpretation by different newspapers is not very likely to make the community feel that it can see in the dark. Press lords like the late Colonel McCormick of the Chicago *Tribune* ("the world's greatest newspaper") may believe that their paper is as necessary as the morning milk and as enlightening to the common sight as a diet of vitaminised carrots; they go to their graves in ignorance of the fact that their readers were not their trusting vassals but bought the paper because they enjoyed it in spite of its pompous pretences. Northcliffe, who had the courage of his crude convictions, said there were only two reasons for buying a paper: curiosity or habit.

And you can hardly blame the Press for taking its role so solemnly when everybody else does too—including the Government. In the U.S. the Press gets cheap postal rates which almost amount to a government subsidy. In Britain, where the Press also gets special rates for telegrams and mailing, the Royal Commission has countersigned the Press's charter

> as the chief agency for instructing the public on the main issues of the day. . . . Democratic society . . . needs a clear and truthful account of events, of their background and their causes; a forum for discussion and informed criticism; and a means whereby individuals and groups can express a point of view or advocate a cause. The responsibility for fulfilling these needs unavoidably rests in large measure upon the Press. . . . In recent years this function has been shared with the radio; but the impermanence of broadcasting, together with the limitations of the quantity and character of controversial material which can be diffused over the air, still leaves the Press in a central position.

This is a counsel of perfection, an ideal description of what the Press is supposed to do which the Press accepts as a description of what it actually does. Nevertheless, even if it falls short of being the wise guide and responsible counsellor it's cracked up to be, the Press has its points as a nervous watchdog. Though many papers take the comfortable view that the Press's role is to echo the people's voice when it's raised and soothe it when it's silent, some "crusading" newspapers are always looking for trouble. Often they find cause for alarm where none exists, or sensationalise a little into a lot, but they can pretty well be counted on to raise the alarm when trouble is really there.

The Press of course claims to be responsible—as an institution and as individual newspapers. In fact, it considers itself almost an extension of government. C. P. Scott, the famous editor who controlled the *Manchester Guardian* for more than 50 years, called the Press "in its way, an instrument of government". "In its way", he said; but only in the sense that the Sunday orators at Marble Arch might be considered an extension of a government that constitutionally tolerates the utmost freedom of speech, so long as sticks and stones don't follow the hard words. No doubt it was the solider elements in the Press that Scott had most in mind. He may have been thinking of the *Manchester Guardian's* long record of loyal opposition—its battle for Home Rule for Ireland, its Nathan-like refusal to condone the South African War. Or the period when the London *Times* was the voice, but thinly disguised, of the Government. Or the times when a newspaper may become the official mouthpiece of government, as the London *Daily Herald* did when the Labour Party was in power.

In the United States, where no political party owns or controls any important newspaper, with the unimportant exception of the Communist *Daily Worker*, the situation is somewhat different. Newspapers there are as partisan as in Britain, but because of the size of the country the papers circulate regionally instead of nationally. This does something to increase their natural jealousy and watchfulness of one another, and makes it less possible for one of them to be "most-favoured" by the administration. They are always jockeying for a more favourable position, however, through their Washington correspondents. These correspondents cultivate prominent Congressmen, Senators, Cabinet officers and officers of the State Department in the hope of getting more or less important and more or less exclusive items of news. And Government officers often use friendly correspondents to "plant" stories in the Press which they don't want to announce officially. This mutual arrangement doesn't always work smoothly. Sometimes the favoured correspondent and his newspaper are attacked by the rest of the Press as Government stooges—a damaging charge if it can be made to stick. Sometimes the trial balloon flops or catches fire, and then the public may get angry with the suspected source or even with the Government itself. Chancy and unsatisfactory as this system may be, it is clearly an instance of the Press making itself a kind of extension of Government, and of the Government making use of the Press as an instrument.

A popular Press with the people behind it, or even one paper of enormous circulation, can sometimes so put the fear of votes into a vote-conscious Government that it will respond to the pressure. Then the sections of the Press that support the Government set up the cry of "irresponsible journalism!"

"Irresponsible" is the dirtiest name one paper can call another. It has become so emotional a term, in fact, that it almost defies definition. "Responsibility" is held by the Press to be the chief of all journalistic virtues. Responsibility to whom, and for what? To the public, for making an honest report of what happened yesterday. That's the theory: but for each paper, in practice, "the public" is its readers; and what *did* happen yesterday? No paper will ever admit that it is or has been irresponsible—under its present management, that is. It may confess to every other sin in the journalistic calendar, but not that one. Few journalists, when sober, will admit it either.

The hero of C. E. Montague's novel, *A Hind Let Loose*, who simultaneously wrote partisan leaders for two opposed papers, has had at least one counterpart in real life: the man who wrote leaders for the New York *Daily News*, which was then pro-New Deal, and also for the *Saturday Evening Post*, which was violently anti-New Deal. His leaders were unsigned, but he publicly admitted writing them, explaining that he was a professional editorial writer and wrote either way for pay. He might also have claimed to be a responsible journalist who was simply exercising his responsibility to two duties—which happened to be diametrically different.

The term "irresponsibility" as applied to the Press, or to certain parts of it, usually seems to mean a fundamental lack of seriousness, a cynical disregard for consistency, callousness about harming individuals and degrading public manners and morals.

> An aspect of . . . sensationalism which has attracted much attention is the intrusion on the privacy of individuals necessary to satisfy the appetite for intimate personal detail about the lives and affairs of people who are, perhaps quite accidentally, in the news. In ordinary circumstances this may be no more than an annoyance to the people concerned, but if they have suffered some personal tragedy it may cause great pain. . . .
>
> The pain given to individuals is, however, only part of the evil of this practice. The greater evil lies in the degradation of public taste which results from the gratification of morbid curiosity, and in the debasement of the professional standards of the journalists who, whether willingly or otherwise, minister to it. . . .

A paper may make sweeping assertions or innuendos about a person or institution or foreign country, and it may continue to make them for several days or even several weeks. This is known as a "crusade". If these assertions or innuendos turn out to be obviously wrong, or fail to catch the readers' interest, the paper may simply drop the subject, with not a word said of apology for having misled its readers or as amends to the reputations it has vilified. If the paper commits an actionable libel and its lawyers admit it, it will settle the case out of court if it can by printing a retraction, as brief and as little humiliating to itself as possible. But a retraction can never undo the harm caused by false statement. A lie can sometimes be nailed, but a lie is amazingly difficult to kill.

A hard-pressed editor is only too well aware of the number of mistakes and misstatements that somehow get printed in his paper, and it sometimes seems to him that he does nothing but publish retractions and apologies. It doesn't seem that way, however, to the insulted and injured—nor to the public. Said the Hutchins Commission: "One of the most effective ways of improving the Press is blocked by the Press itself. By a kind of unwritten law the Press ignores the errors and misrepresentations, the lies and scandals, of which its members are guilty." This too is an extreme statement, but it also has "a substantial element of truth".

In theory (and in law) responsibility in the Press is concentrated on a few top men; but in practice it is distributed so widely that in most cases no one person can actually be held responsible. This situation was viewed with alarm by the Hutchins Commission:

> The element of personal responsibility, which is of the essence of the organisation of such professions as law and medicine, is missing in communications [i.e., the Press]. Here the writer works for an employer, and the employer, not the writer, takes the responsibility. . . . Charles Beard could say with accuracy that "in its origin, freedom of the Press had little or nothing to do with truth telling . . . most of the early papers were partisan sheets devoted to savage attacks on party opponents. . . . Freedom of the Press meant the right to be just or unjust, partisan or non-partisan, true or false, in news column or editorial column." Today, this former legal privilege wears the aspect of social irresponsibility. The Press

must know that its faults and errors have ceased to be private vagaries and have become public dangers.

For one misstatement that is "corrected" (i.e., admitted) a hundred are preserved in newspaper files and repeated again and again, thus helping [illegible]alsify the history of our day. The only recourse against this [illegible]t of damage is in the vigilance and sense of public responsib[illegible]y of the Press itself.

The word "public" is [illegible]e key. By the terms of that unwritten charter which the Press [illegible]aims to hold, it undertakes a responsibility to the *public* to g[illegible]e a true report, to the best of its ability, of what's going on in [illegible]e world. In the words of C. P. Scott: "[A newspaper's] prim[illegible]ry office is the gathering of news. At the peril of its soul it must [illegible]e that the supply is not tainted. Neither in what it gives, nor [illegible] what it does not give, nor in the mode of presentation must the unclouded face of truth suffer wrong. Comment is free, b[illegible]t facts are sacred."

No newspaper will admit that it feels less than the full load of public responsibility which the Press as a whole has undertaken. But the performance of the popular Press gives the game away. Its readers do not as yet constitute the whole nation, or even include the better-informed and more intelligent parts of it, yet the popular Press acts as if this educated minority were negligible, and seems to feel that its only responsibility is towards its own readers.

As for the Press's relation to government (still taking the Press at the popular estimate), it may be thought of as an extension of government in the same way that a brickbat may be considered an extension of a window, or as a pat may be considered an extension of a back.

The Press claims that it is an educative force. Some journalists would go further and claim that newspapers are the most important and most effective schoolrooms there are—far more effective than the smattering of formal education most people get in school. And it's true that a tremendous amount of information, on practically every subject on and off the curriculum, gets into the papers. When Carr van Anda was managing editor of the New York *Times* he published the complete text of Einstein's First Field Theory. Few if any of the *Times*' readers could understand one word or mathematical symbol of it, but there it was.

The education offered by newspapers is not systematic, as formal schools try to be, but every newspaper does in a sense give instruction in different subjects, keyed to the interests and intellectual level of its readers. The *Manchester Guardian* is a daily compendium of modern and current history and politics, theoretical and applied science, economics, contemporary literature and art, and on occasion writes about archaeology, ancient history, philosophy and engineering as well. For its huge and unruly class the *Daily Mirror* too, using mostly capital letters and a simplified syllabus, chalks up a good deal of information on the blackboard: current history and politics, economics, general knowledge, social and emotional problems. Both papers are a mine of useful facts on cooking, dressmaking and fashions.

But newspapers give lectures, not classes, and their readers are choosy. There are no penalties for cuts or for leaving the lecture before the end. There are no exams, and no exact way of telling how much the student-reader is absorbing. This is a constant anxiety to the newspaper-teacher. "Not what you get on to the page but what you get off the page into the reader's mind" is what counts, said *Time*, didactic from the start. Newspaper editors sometimes try to reassure themselves by "readership tests", which show how many people are reading which parts of the paper. But the most reliable indicator of whether readers are paying attention is the circulation, and next to that, letters to the editor.

The quality Press, which was first in the field by several generations, was written for an already educated group of readers. It didn't attempt to raise their educational level, but to meet it. The popular Press, whose early days go back only to the 1890s, aimed deliberately to catch the eye of the *nouveaux riches* of literacy, the enormous and growing audience of readers brought into being by the spread of free education. Up to that time this audience either couldn't read or couldn't afford to buy a newspaper. In 1829, when newspapers were much dearer than they are now, each copy of the average London paper was read by 30 people. The simplified and sensational penny Press of the 1890s was cut to the pattern of pleasing brand-new readers. Its primary aim was to interest them and keep on interesting them. Its claim to be an educative force was a defensive after-thought.

Afterthought or no, however, the claim must be allowed. Since most readers of the popular Press read nothing else, they depend on it for most of their information about the world. The educative effort of the quality Press has tended to preserve standards of education that already existed, while the popular Press has tended to set up new standards where none existed before. Everyone now "has a right" to "be educated", and the general effect has been to lower the overall level of education, since more people now regard themselves as educated, measuring themselves against the lower standard of the popular Press. As an old-school British statesman once remarked, one of the most palpable results of popular education has been that dirty words are to be found rather lower down the walls of public conveniences than they used to be.

The Press claims to be a reflection of the national state of culture. This claim seems to me irrefutable. The Press likes to think of itself as a bulletin board, but it's not. It's much more like a newsreel theatre, in which oil-tank fires, politicians at microphones, animated cartoons, travelogues, fashion shows and sporting events flicker one after another across the screen. Nobody would claim that a newsreel theatre gives a true and adequate report of what's going on in the world. But nobody could deny, either, that it's a true reflection of what goes on, in bits and pieces. In the same way the Press is a true reflection: it just can't help being.

If by "culture" you mean show-pieces—singular, aristocratic

achievements—then the Press of a nation doesn't adequately reflect its culture. But I take culture to include all aspects of life, and in that sense a nation's culture can't be hidden. You can't say, "Look at this—but don't look at that." Hollywood isn't its best films or even its prize-winners, but all its films togethe To a foreigner travelling in the U.S., and even more to peo who have never been there, the hallmark of U.S. civilisat is not its books, painting or architecture, but its "standard f living". And the thing that got Americans to that high mate l level and keeps them there is mass production—mass produ on of what economists call consumer goods.

The popu r Press is part of mass production, in both Britain and the U.S. nd a very important part. It's not only the chief advertiser of nsumer goods, but the loudest champion of "progress"—b which is meant an ever-rising standard of living. Thus it c n't help being a reflection of national culture. In the popular ress the masses of the nation see their own tastes, aspirations and fears continually reflected. So do the educated minority, nd they don't like what they see. They think these tastes are chaotic, the aspirations vulgar, and the fears hysterical. But however much the educated minority and their quality Press may deprecate the national culture, it still exists.

The Royal Commission on the Press found some encouraging things to say about the popular Press in Britain and, a little back-handedly, about the culture it reflects:

> [The popular paper] is remarkable value for money. We can think of no other product, equally expensive to produce, which is sold for so small a sum. The readers of the penny[1] newspaper clearly find in it something that satisfies their reading needs. They find a brightly coloured kaleidoscopic picture of the world day by day. They find exciting incidents at home and abroad; they find pathos and tragedy mingled with sentiment and comedy; they find personal gossip about the great or the notorious and about people in the news who

[1] Now 2*d.*, which is still cheap.

are neither great nor notorious but have caught the popular imagination for the moment; they find well-produced photographs of people or places. Great affairs of national or international importance may not always get the space or the dispassionate treatment that is their due, but they are not neglected, nor are serious features lacking, even if the lighter predominate.

The Press claims that it supplies daily entertainment to millions. It doesn't make this claim very loudly; it doesn't want to emphasise this part of its performance. All newspaper editors try to put out "a good paper" every day. Papers like the *Daily Mirror* know what that means and admit it: an exciting, interesting, *entertaining* paper. They know they can't depend on the luck of the news; they can't count on a daily disaster, scandal, murder or love affair. So the paper is built around a framework of features, including, very decidedly, strip cartoons and manufactured "news" (speculation, gossip, rumour, chit-chat). The constant aim of the mass-circulation editor is to enhance what news there is, and to make up for what news there isn't.

The word 'news' has come to mean something different from important new information. When a journalist says that a certain event is news, he does not mean that it is important in itself. Often it is; but about as often it is not. The journalist means by news something that has happened within the last few hours which will attract the attention of the customers.

The *Daily Mirror* knows to a T what's news and what isn't, in this sense. It's out to attract attention, to get itself looked at and sometimes even read, at least partly. To do the job, it has to make itself a daily entertainment, a kind of magazine with something unexpected or amusing in even its regular features. The *Mirror's* big boss, Cecil King, knows what his paper is doing and why. In 1955 he told his shareholders: "Though some newspapers do not yet seem aware of the fact, the advent of radio altered the character of newspapers from that of purveyors of news towards that of daily magazines."[1] In the *Mirror's* view of itself, it's a daily cocktail with fizz in it. Taken first thing in the morning, at the start of another grey working day, it gives the reader a little spurt of liveliness—and makes him look forward to another cocktail tomorrow.

The customers must be attracted. This open secret about the fundamental nature of the Press has been discovered by the *Mirror* and exploited to a fare-ye-well. But even the *Mirror* wouldn't come right out and say that entertainment is its only aim, or its chief one. No, even the most blatant tabloids insist that they are really, first and foremost, serious, crusading journals, vigilant guardians of democracy, etc., etc. And so they are, in a way. But—"first and foremost"?

The secret is still denied as a libel or denounced as a heresy by the Press as a whole. Yet the Press has followed the *Mirror's* lead in coating the pill of hard news with the sugar of entertainment; strip cartoons, gossip about movie stars, sports heroes, society figures, humorous columns, jokes, "light" news items, pictures of beautiful landscape or beautiful girls, fiction, astrology columns, advice to the lovelorn, crossword puzzles, chess problems, competitions—the list is long and getting longer. Even the London *Times*, that strait-laced embodiment of journalistic dignity, plays the game according to its lights: consciously in its famous Fourth Leader, wreathing its lithe proboscis to make the reader mirth,[2] and often unconsciously in its Personal column, its letters-to-the-editor, and its political reporting, which is frequently and amusingly "slanted". The *Mirror* thinks the *Times* doesn't know what it's doing. Maybe

[1] This discovery was announced earlier in the U.S. by the Hutchins Commission in *A Free and Responsible Press*: "The American newspaper is now as much a medium of entertainment, specialised information, and advertising as it is of news."

[2] " . . . the unwieldy elephant,
To make them mirth, used all his might, and wreathed
His lithe proboscis. . . ."

Paradise Lost

not; but the *Times* too knows what its customers like. The *Times* too studies how to rouse its own readers, and how to cater for them.

What's the purpose of a newspaper? The answer depends on who's talking. First, the "official line". The avowed purpose of a newspaper is to supply news to its community and to be a social and/or political force. You get that official line in some of the slogans newspapers have taken for themselves—"More light", "Let the people know", "An informed democracy is a healthy democracy", "Forward with the people".

The Hutchins Commission took this line in describing the needs which it considered that the Press is supposed to supply:

> Our society needs an accurate, truthful account of the day's events. We need to know what goes on in our own locality, region and nation. We need reliable information about all other countries. We need to supply other countries with such information about ourselves. We need a market place for the exchange of comment and criticism regarding public affairs. We need to reproduce on a gigantic scale the open argument which characterised the village gathering two centuries ago. We need to project across all groups, regions, and nations a picture of the constituent elements of the modern world. We need to clarify the aims and ideals of our community and every other.

The Report proceeded to lambaste the Press because

> much of what passes [in the Press] for public discussion is sales talk. . . . The news is being twisted by the emphasis on firstness, on the novel and sensational; by the personal interests of owners; and by pressure groups. Too much of the regular output of the Press consists of a miscellaneous succession of stories and images which have no relation to the typical lives of real people anywhere. Too often the result is meaninglessness, flatness, distortion, and the perpetuation

> of misunderstanding among widely scattered groups whose only contact is through these media. . . . When we look at the Press as a whole . . . we must conclude that it is not meeting the needs of our society.

Another answer is that a newspaper is simply a tool in the hands of its owner. This is the view of a brilliant ex-newspaperman, Claud Cockburn:

> It seemed to me that a newspaper is always a weapon in somebody's hands, and I never could see why it should be shocking that the weapon should be used in what its owner conceived to be his best interests. The hired journalist, I thought, ought to realise that he is partly in the entertainment business and partly in the advertising business—advertising either goods, or a cause, or a government. He just has to make up his mind whom he wants to entertain, and what he wants to advertise. The humbug and hypocrisy of the Press begin only when newspapers pretend to be "impartial" or "servants of the public". And this only becomes dangerous as well as laughable when the public is fool enough to believe it.

The real purpose of a newspaper is to survive. Its aim is to keep on keeping on, either just barely, if it must, or expanding, if it can. And it has to appear every day or every week, whether it wants to or not, whether it really has anything to say or not. At the San Francisco meeting that began the United Nations, "on many days . . . there was nothing to report. But the reporters had to send in their stories. Somehow there had to be news."

The primary purpose of a newspaper is to survive. To do that, it must keep its personality alive. Its secondary purpose is to entertain and instruct. All newspapers try to instruct their readers, according to their lights. All newspapers try to entertain them, according to their character.

The Journalist

Many people consider a journalist a disappointed writer. Few journalists would agree: they're more likely to think that the shoe is on the other foot. They write every day and get paid every week and most of what they write gets printed. Can most "writers" say as much? But writing journalists are not the whole show in journalism. They are charter members of a club that has had to open its doors to all kinds of other people: news-photographers, feature-writers, strip-cartoonists, book-reviewers, theatre critics, pollsters, pattern-makers, sob-sisters, writers of hints on gardening, on refurbishing old houses, choosing a hobby, building a boat in the cellar, etc., etc.—every imaginable kind of specialist and trained seal. The journalist today is anyone who gets regularly published in a newspaper.

Then there are the bosses, big and little, whose contributions rarely appear in print, whose writing is confined to technical reports or inter-office memoranda: the publishers, editors, advertising and circulation managers. According to them, they are the ones who really count, for they control the Press. The editor of the Richmond (Virginia) *Times-Despatch*, a man gloriously named Virginius Dabney, had this to say about his colleagues on the business side: "The typical American publisher considers the important part of the paper to be the business management, and is convinced that so long as high salaries and lavish expenditures are made available to that management, the editorial department can drag along under a schedule of too much work and too little pay. Of course, such a publisher sees that the editorials in his paper are 'sound', which is to say that they conform to his own weird idea of society, and are largely unreadable."

It would be silly to deny that certain publishers exert a great deal of influence on papers which they consider their property, because they own a controlling share in the paper's stock; or that these publishers and proprietors are often ignorant and sometimes mad. But luckily for j rnalism, and perhaps for democracy, no paper is ever altogether under control, or under the control of one man, in spite of the fearful scenes and outcries made by the man who imagines that he does or should control it.

No, it's neither the proprietor nor his pals who really count most in j rnalism, but the men who do the actual writing. And ho re they doing? "The quality of the Press depends in large pa upon the capacity and independence of the working membe in the lower ranks. At the present time their wages and pr stige are low and their tenure precarious." They were not t ined for their jobs. They learned their trade by working at i Whereas, says the Hutchins Commission, "the kind of tra ing a journalist needs most today is not training in the tri ks and machinery of the trade. If he is to be a competent j dge of public affairs, he needs the broadest and most liberal ducation."

Generally speaking, a journalist nowadays is a tradesman. Most of the journalists I have known could hardly have cared less about the aims or even the direction of the job we all shared. I'm not talking about the best nor the worst, but about the majority. All of these were keen on their jobs; they took pride in strict standards of performance; they held to a rigid code of professional ethics: never invent, never suppress awkward facts, never divulge a "source", etc. They wrote as well as they could under the circumstances—sometimes appalling circumstances. They went to great pains to get their facts and figures right. But they never bothered their heads about the sum total or about the problem itself: what journalism is in fact, what it is supposed to be or might be, how well or how badly it's being done. Some felt no interest in the editorial policy of their paper; others were at odds with it but said, "Where can you get a better job?"; most of them wrote for an audience of one—the editor. Some played a kind of game whose purpose was to get into print, under the editor's nose, as much as possible that would make a monkey of his views and the paper's principles.

Did none of them regard themselves as responsible to the public-at-large, for whom supposedly they were reporting the facts of daily life? Yes, a few. The editor himself was apt to be one who felt responsible to the public—sometimes even to a wider public than the paper's readers. And many, perhaps a sizeable minority of the men who wrote for a journal of high character and proud traditions, an aristocrat of the Press like the New York *Times*, shared or at least approved its sense of public mission. There were also the sea-green incorruptibles who acknowledged no authority but some inner light of their own. These rarities were in journalism but never altogether of it. They gave their editors more trouble than anybody but they made the whole undertaking worthwhile.

But the majority did their day's work and let it go at that. No doubt the same holds true for other trades and professions. Those who can, do; the ones who have time and inclination to criticise are on the sidelines. But even as a working journalist I sometimes wondered: does journalism actually do more harm than good? Is it, as advertised, a necessary instrument of democracy? Or is it a handicap to civilisation? Is it an extension of government and an educative force, or a sower of chaos and a corrupter of youth? Does it in fact further understanding between nations, or foment discord? Does it give the news of the world, or the gossip of the village? Is it the clouded mirror of our days, or a warped sounding-board that sends out distorted and lying echoes?

The working journalist usually has no time for these doubts.

PART II

THE DAILY MIRROR: NORTHCLIFFE TO KING

"*Is the Prince of Wales* [later Edward VII] *known as Tum-Tum?*"

"*Yes. He is given the name by a limited circle of intimates because of the pleasing rotundity of his person.*"

This titbit appeared in a weekly paper called *Answers to Correspondents*, in the late 80s of the last century. In spite of the Victorian language, these 28 words contained the very gist of popular journalism. Was it news? Well, of a sort. True? That hardly mattered. The real point of this "disclosure" was that it was amusing, shocking, titillating, and calculated to entertain a certain class of reader. Perhaps more than one class. The smart young man who started *Answers* was named Alfred Harmsworth. He was 23. Like Tum-Tum, he later changed his status and title, and when he died at 57 was famous throughout the semi-literate world as the first (and only) Lord Northcliffe.

Alfred Harmsworth, born in a suburb of Dublin in 1865, was the eldest of fourteen children: seven boys and seven girls. His father was a barrister, his mother a woman of forceful character. Money was scarce in the Harmsworth household, and Alfred never got to a university. Instead he went to work at a series of jobs that were mainly in the field of journalism or publishing, and he started his independent career in Fleet Street with one simple idea: to make money. When he died in 1922 his will was proved at £3½ million, a sizeable profit from the much greater amounts he had pumped back into the business and poured down various drains.

Not because he was interested in journalism in itself, but because he wanted to discover the weaknesses and possibilities of a market he intended to dominate, Harmsworth had made a careful study of nineteenth-century British newspapers. He had found out two things that interested him very much: first, that the staid monotony of the late Victorian Press was an exception to an earlier rule of sensational news and blatant advertisements; second, that the gradual abolition of taxes on newspapers and the spread of free education had for the first time made it possible to sell cheap papers to a potentially enormous and growing public.

One Fleet Street publication, *Tit-Bits*, had already pointed the way; but Harmsworth saw that more clearly than its own editor: "The Board Schools are turning out hundreds of thousands of boys and girls annually who are anxious to read. They do not care for the ordinary newspaper. They have no interest in society, but they will read anything which is simple and is sufficiently interesting. The man who has produced this *Tit-Bits* has got hold of a bigger thing than he imagines. He is only at the beginning of a development which is going to change the whole face of journalism."

Harmsworth "felt, with perfect confidence and with perfect justice, that he could cater for tens of thousands—and, as self-confidence grew, for millions—of people who were conventional without being cultured, and who were demanding, more and more, to be amused." The trick was to catch the audience, and he tried all kinds of stunts. One day a tramp on the Embankment told him that all he wanted in the world was a pound a week for life. In its next number *Answers* offered a pound a week for life to the reader who came nearest guessing the exact amount of money in the Bank of England on a certain day. The circulation of *Answers* immediately shot up.

Alfred's second brother, Harold, had joined him and proved to be a financial wizard. On the success of *Answers* the brothers founded the Amalgamated Press, which was to become the world's largest periodical publishing business. Soon their profits were up to £50,000 a year. They decided to invade the field of daily newspapers. After buying the moribund *Evening News* (1894) and reorganising it into a success, in 1896 they started a new halfpenny morning paper, the *Daily Mail*.

"The busy man's newspaper", as Alfred Harmsworth called it, shook Fleet Street to its dusty cellars. With Alfred's nose for newsmongering and Harold's head for figures, the two brothers made the contemporary methods of journalism look very old-fashioned. Like *Time*, a generation later, the *Daily Mail* was based on the conviction that the Press was a stodgy mess and didn't know what news was (but Alfred Harmsworth knew: news was what interested *him*) and above all was boring and long-winded. The *Daily Mail* spent fortunes on cable services, to get news faster and fresher, on famous names to write despatches and special articles, on stunts and enterprises of all kinds. When news was dull it was condensed. The very first number printed a leader hailing the future of the almost unknown and unregarded motor car. By the time of the Boer War the *Daily Mail* was a household word in Britain, and selling 600,000 copies a day.

When Alfred Harmsworth left the *Daily Mail* office the night the first number went to press, he said exultantly, "We've struck a gold mine!" And so he had; but what was he to do with his money? He wanted to do something with it: he wanted to exercise power. That meant, in England, political power. But to have that kind of power in England meant, in turn, that one had to be respected. Success was not enough; some kinds of success, in fact, were hardly respectable. As Lord Northcliffe, he was soon to have his achievement officially confirmed by a peerage, but that would not satisfy him either. He could tickle or alarm a large public, he could bully and terrify his subordinates, he could impress or at least annoy a Prime Minister, but he could never get what he most wanted: the power he thought he would possess if he were recognised as genuinely respectable. His life became an increasingly furious struggle to win this recognition by the only methods he knew: force and guile.

That struggle was to come to a head when he bought control of the *Times* in 1908 and for 14 years tried in vain to re-shape the paper into an instrument of his personal policy. But an early indication that the struggle had begun was the launching of the *Daily Mirror* in 1903. The first number of the *Daily Mirror* was heralded by an unprecedented, nation-wide fanfare of advertising. The paper itself, however, was a sharp contrast to the sensational *Daily Mail:* it was a woman's newspaper, "written by gentlewomen for gentlewomen".[1] And it was a near-disaster. The preliminary advertising, and Harmsworth's reputation, were enough to sell out the first number of 265,000 copies, at 1*d.* a copy; then the sales nose-dived. When they were down to 25,000, Harmsworth's instinct for self-preservation overcame his stubborn vanity. He cut the price to ½*d.*, fired the gentlewomanly staff, changed the paper's character completely, and featured news photographs. Circulation began to climb again. Harmsworth admitted—or rather boasted, for great men are able to see even their blunders as Pyrrhic victories—that he lost £100,000 on the venture before he decided to cut his losses.

To get the *Mirror's* circulation up and keep it climbing, Harmsworth tried all the tricks of the trade he had learned with the *Mail*. These were a few of them: publicising a 2,000-mile motor trip (this was in 1904) in which the car's engine never stopped; a photograph of sunrise over the Alps taken from a balloon; prizes for swimming the Channel, for beauty competitions, for the most beautiful baby; wireless tests from a plane (1910). By 1914 the *Mirror's* circulation was well over a million. But by that time Harmsworth (now Lord Northcliffe) had lost interest in the paper. The *Daily Mail*, which always remained his favourite creation, and the *Times*, with whose Editor and editorial policies he was locked in devious struggle, were more than enough to occupy him. And he had recently made another blunder in acquiring a Manchester printing

[1] The first number bore this Dedication:

> So now the Mirror of the day,
> The gift most lavish, and the last,
> Lies waiting, Woman, in your way,
> To show your face, to hold the past,
> To catch each ray the time outpours
> And flash it back. The glass is yours.

plant for the *Mirror* on which he was losing £600 a week. He sold control of the *Mirror* to his brother Harold.

Like most of the Press lords who have followed him, Northcliffe misunderstood the nature of the power he could wield, overestimated its extent, and never really knew what to do with it. He realised that with papers like the *Daily Mail* and the *Daily Mirror* he could never hope to reach the people he most wanted to influence: the "Westminster square mile", the real rulers of England. As inevitably as Napoleon was drawn towards Moscow, this unsatisfied craving drew him to the attempted conquest of the *Times*. On those alien and freezing steppes his native wit faltered and foundered. But it was a bloody and protracted campaign, whose eloquent memorials, like the tombstones in a war cemetery, can be read in the *History of the Times*.

At first Northcliffe kept to the pretence that his invasion of the paper was not an invasion at all, merely the friendly tour of an allied monarch. It was a pretence he could not keep up for long. As the *Times*' historian says: "It is possible to discern if not to define Northcliffe's plan to increase his power. It was a plan to master the *Times* by mastering the principal members of the staff. He followed it consistently and subtly until his death. . . . He made it a point in his programme to be quite as well informed concerning the staff as the Editor and Manager. He was proud of his knowledge and openly boasted of 'my spies' and 'my ferrets'."

In 1914, his telegraphed orders from abroad, where his bank account, ill health and increasing hypochondria took him for longer and longer periods, were still in the guise of requests: "Humbly beg for light leading article daily until I return—Chief." By 1922 they were more outspoken: "I SHALL GIVE YOU ALL HELL WHEN I GET BACK—CHIEF."

The beautifully educated journalists who wrote and edited the *Times* were fascinated and appalled by this crude yet subtle barbarian from Outer Fleet Street. The opinion they have recorded of him as a person would not have pleased him:

"Northcliffe, at once more elementary and more experienced than his brother [Rothermere], was guided by instinct, intuition and mood, not by principle, consistency or reason. . . . The truth was that at this time [1922] Northcliffe's health, physical and other, varied. One day he was wilful, venomous and erratic, the next day cool, kindly and consistent. At will he could be one or the other."

When Northcliffe wanted to get rid of Wickham Steed, then Editor of the *Times*, but didn't quite dare to fire him outright, he summoned Steed to his villa in the south of France. "He began his attack on Steed by flattering him. He then tried, and nearly succeeded in the effort, to break Steed's nerve by belabouring him and his family with every kind of indecent insult. With great strength of mind Steed cut him short by saying, 'These are not things that I can listen to. Goodbye.' As events were to fall out, this was the last that the Editor saw of Northcliffe."

Though Northcliffe never succeeded in bending the *Times* to his will, he did leave his mark on the paper, and the *Times* acknowledges it: "Unquestionably the greatest popular journalist of his time. . . . The *Times* was not his creation but he re-created it. Yet he neither understood it nor felt at home in it. He came to it too late. He had long admired and coveted its influence, and wished to possess it for himself as the crown of his career. . . ."

Northcliffe did not understand the *Times*, but he knew a stuffy newspaper when he saw one. His constant nagging, urging and bullying had the effect of making the *Times* less stuffy. His pressure for a daily light leader resulted in the famous "Fourth Leader", now a *Times* tradition. And by bringing off the daring gamble of dropping the price of the paper from 2*d.* to 1*d.*, he lifted the *Times*' circulation at a swoop from 47,000 to 145,000. That gain gave the paper a new lease of life which it never lost, and this stroke of publishing genius was Northcliffe's single-handed achievement, as the *Times* handsomely allows: "The operation had succeeded beyond his hopes against great odds and the entire credit was his."

But Northcliffe's delusions of grandeur, an occupational disease to which lords of the Press seem to be peculiarly prone, were notable. Geoffrey Dawson, an Editor of the *Times* who parted company with him, thought that he "enormously overrates the influence of his own papers". A joke from an earlier era was revived: "Have you heard? The Prime Minister has resigned and Northcliffe has sent for the King." In the rivalry between Lloyd George and Asquith, Northcliffe had supported Lloyd George; when Lloyd George became Prime Minister, Northcliffe thought he had him in his pocket. There was a showdown, thus described by Lloyd George: "I put up with him for four years. The break had to come—when he wanted to dictate to me. As Prime Minister I could not have it. Northcliffe thought he could run the country. I could not allow that. It was a good thing for me that I did not get turned out while he was alive or he would have claimed he had done it."

It was the considered opinion of his colleagues on the *Times* that Northcliffe wanted above all "the absolutely unfettered, independent exercise of personal power through the Press". Did this ambition, and his waking dream that he had partly attained it, spring from a deep unsureness in himself, almost an inferiority complex? It seems likely. Once, in reminiscent mood, he said: "I have suffered from one disability throughout my career. You would never guess it. . . . I suffer from the fact that I was not at Oxford." On another occasion he was charmed by a young lady who told him she was bored by London social life and would like to be a journalist; whereupon he ordered one of his editors to hire her at £20 a week, and to justify himself said: "Have you looked her up in the *Peerage*? She is a very high-up young person. I am about number 3,000, having got there after much pushing and shoving. But she's much higher up than that."

The popular Press of our day is a memorial to Northcliffe: he was its begetter. Would he have acknowledged his offspring? Perhaps not altogether willingly. Some of the commoner practices of tabloid journalism—the screaming headlines, the deafening black type, the jigsaw lay-outs, the "cheesecake", the strip cartoons; even more, the deliberate vulgarism, the more brutal invasions of privacy in the ruthless search for "human interest"—these might well have seemed to him a horrible caricature of his methods. He wanted liveliness and brightness, but he thought there were limits. One of his memos to the *Daily Mail* read: "I am afraid our paper was getting stodgy again after the war. We have got it on the right lines now, and have gone to about the limit of brightness. Be brig but dignified."

In Northcliffe's own day, dignity was not one of the reco nised attributes of his papers—except for the *Times*, which was never really "his". And though he improved the *Times*' material position, the fact of his relation with it subtly damaged that newspaper's reputation without enhancing his own. His favourite, the *Daily Mail*, was popular not because its readers had confidence in its integrity but because it entertained them.

The *Daily Mirror*, the *Mail's* less-favoured younger sister, was unmistakably a member of the same undignified family. In its early days, when the *Mirror* was full of news pictures, Lord Salisbury remarked that Mr. Harmsworth had invented a paper for those who could read but could not think, and another for those who could see but could not read.

In 1914 Harold Harmsworth (he became Lord Rothermere the same year) bought the *Mirror* from his brother, and under his management the paper continued to grow and make money. But Rothermere's treatment of a newspaper was markedly different from his brother's. Northcliffe regarded his papers as his personal weapons, to be fitted to the shape of his hand; to Rothermere, a newspaper was a property. (The story goes that when Northcliffe bought control of the *Times* he asked his brother to take a look at the paper's books; Rothermere did, and burst into tears.) Northcliffe was an editorial boss, concerned with any and every aspect of policy, make-up, personnel, etc., and apt to jab his stubby finger into any editorial pie at whatever stage of its baking. Rothermere was a proprietor, a "front offices" boss, whose main concern was the balance sheets. Though Northcliffe was physically absent from London for far greater periods than his brother, he kept his editors up to the mark—or frantically searching for a new one—by telegrams and telephone calls. Rothermere stayed in closer touch with his papers, but he was really more of an absentee boss than Northcliffe.

In prosperous times an established publishing property can, as they say, "run itself" under this kind of management. The times were prosperous, and the *Mirror* was by now established. Rothermere followed his talents and concentrated on developing the paper's distribution system, strengthening its financial position by shrewd investments; he bought other newspapers, in London and the provinces, and started a Sunday paper, the *Sunday Pictorial*. In 1927 he moved the *Mirror* and the *Pictorial* into a new plant (called Geraldine House, after his mother), "the last word in up-to-date newspaper efficiency". The grandeurs and glories of Geraldine House—and for their day they were no less—were characteristic of Rothermere's concern for his golden-egg geese: he thought they deserved every material advantage, within sound book-keeping reason.

By 1928 he controlled 14 daily and Sunday newspapers, and he would have been a strange Press lord if he had not felt that itch to influence public opinion which, sooner or later, overcomes the successful businessman-turned-journalist. As an editorial tyrant he was less impetuous than his brother but no less prejudiced and pig-headed, and he lacked Northcliffe's genius for vulgarity; his editorial notions were usually wrong and almost always dull.

Under his heavy but uncertain hand the *Mirror* zigzagged from Liberal to rabid anti-Socialist, supported the Conservatives but attacked Baldwin, for whom Rothermere's early admiration had turned to hate. The *Mirror* praised Mussolini and hailed Hitler, and even gave Oswald Mosley and his Black Shirts a round of applause. It cried that "squandermania" was ruining the country—and kept on so about it that its readers yawned. The older he grew, the gloomier and more pessimistic Rothermere became about the state of the world. The state of the *Mirror*, he thought, was just as bad; and in 1931 he gave up control and sold his shares on the Stock Exchange. In 1914, when he bought the paper, its circulation had been well over a million; after 17 years of his rule it had dropped to just under a million.

For the next few years the *Mirror* wandered in limbo. Nobody in particular owned it, nobody in particular ran it, a dwindling crowd of nobodies-in-particular read it. It kept going by sheer inertia. In the words of its present Editorial Director, Hugh Cudlipp, the paper "had no identity, no personality of its own, no *raison d'être*". At this low ebb two men got control of the *Mirror* and remade it completely. The two men could hardly have been more different, but they made an effective team.

One of them, Cecil Harmsworth King, nephew of Rothermere and Northcliffe, had entered Fleet Street from the top. The other, Harry Guy Bartholomew, had come in at the bottom. King was shy, cold, calculating, with much of his uncle Rothermere's business sense. He had been educated at Winchester and Christ Church, Oxford, had served a brief term as a reporter on a Glasgow paper, then went to the advertising department of the *Daily Mail*. Three years later Rothermere shifted him to the *Mirror*. Soon he was Advertising and Financial Director of the *Mirror* and *Pictorial*.

Bartholomew had never been a reporter or a writing journalist, but he knew all about newspapers; and he got his education on the job. He had worked his way up from the engraving department and became a factotum, expert and boss in the field of news pictures. Northcliffe had made him a director at the age of 28. Bartholomew was as hot-headed as King was cold, and full of frustrated ideas on how a popular paper should be run. When he was finally given editorial control and was free to experiment, his "tabloid revolution" not only gave a new look to the *Mirror* but to the whole of popular journalism.

King's role in their partnership was to back up Bartholomew

in any experiment that succeeded or gave promise of succeeding. The yardstick of success was rising circulation. King acted as a buffer between Bartholomew and the timider or more antagonistic directors, and occasionally, when he himself thought Bartholomew was going too fast or cutting a corner too sharply, as a brake.

The first change Bartholomew made in the *Mirror* was in its type: he introduced the heavy black letters (sans serif) that are now a tabloid trademark. He "livened up" the format of the pages, shifted the emphasis from news to brighter and breezier features, more strip cartoons. The idea behind these changes was the most fundamental change of all: to cut loose from the *Mirror's* middle-aged, middle-class readers and to capture a new and larger audience, the working class—and the younger ones (19-25) at that. To succeed in this Bartholomew had to give the *Mirror* a new personality; and he did. Behind the bedizened make-up and the jangling costume jewellery a personality emerged: warm, colourful, crude but kindly, often jolly, always downright, with no patience for big words or complex ideas, prone to sudden angers and belligerent questions, irreverent of clerical or mundane authority but a firm believer in the sufficiency of its own decency and common sense—and in its readers'—a vulgar extravert, definitely not a lady but an old girl who was not born yesterday and who knew her way around.

As this new, lusty, sensational *Mirror* grew and prospered, it attracted a lively staff of ambitious young men, whom it paid well and promoted. Soon the *Mirror* was no longer at the bottom of the London popular dailies but shouldering its way to the top. Beaverbrook's *Daily Express* saw its long pre-eminence challenged, and fought in vain to hold its lead.

The duel between the *Express* and the *Mirror* lasted about twelve years. It would probably not have lasted that long had it not been for wartime restrictions on newsprint and the consequent "pegging" of newspaper circulations until the war was over. When free competition for readers was again possible, the

Mirror began to beat the *Express*. In the race to please readers, the *Mirror* had a bigger potential audience and a surer formula.

Ever since he got control of the *Express* in 1922 and of the *Evening Standard* a year later, Beaverbrook had tried—and with far more success than Northcliffe—to use his papers as personal weapons, to serve his own ideas and prejudices. Before the Royal Commission on the Press he testified with great frankness: "I run the paper purely for the purpose of making propaganda, and with no other motive." Unluckily for him, his propaganda almost always ran counter to the trend of popular feeling. In mass journalism the unpopular side is the wrong side, and from this point of view Beaverbrook was usually wrong. As a leader in the *Mirror* once noted with delight: "No cause is truly lost until it has been championed by Lord Beaverbrook." Furthermore, his whimsical habit of hiring able journalists (like David Low, Frank Owen, Michael Foot, Tom Driberg) regardless of how much their opinions or convictions clashed with his own policies and of giving them, however temporarily, some freedom of expression in his papers, did not tend to clarify his propaganda or make it more effective.

Beaverbrook set the *Express* to stem the prevailing stream of events; Cecil King let the *Mirror* ride with the tide. The *Express* backed the Old Guard and refused to surrender the Empire; the *Mirror* joined the march of the working class and cried, "Forward with the People!" The result was inevitable: in spite of its not always dignified brightness, the *Express* began to seem reactionary, the *Mirror* progressive. In 1949 the *Mirror's* circulation topped the *Express's* and has kept well ahead ever since.

Two years later Cecil King parted with Bartholomew and took over the title of Chairman of the *Mirror* and *Pictorial* companies. The usual polite official statements were issued on both sides. King thus became the biggest frog in Fleet Street. As Chairman of Daily Mirror Newspapers Ltd. and Sunday Pictorial Newspapers Ltd. he controlled a vast publishing enterprise, stretching from forests and paper mills in Newfoundland to newspapers in West Africa and radio stations in Australia. The heart and capital of this empire was the *Daily Mirror* itself, the sensational left-wing tabloid that had attained the largest circulation of any daily newspaper in the world.[1]

Forward with the People

The *Daily Mirror* is a national newspaper—i.e., it circulates all over the United Kingdom.[2] Its 5 million daily copies are printed in London and Manchester simultaneously. Late every night and early every morning, six days a week (the *Mirror* does not come out on Sunday), its various editions, six in all, are carried by train, van, bicycle and newsagent's boy to readers and newspaper stalls all over the country. Since Britain is geographically small and densely populated, newspapers printed in London, or in branch printing plants in Manchester and Glasgow, can reach all but the remotest parts of the country by breakfast-time next morning. And there is no competition from foreign newspapers.

At Geraldine House in London the first edition of the *Daily Mirror* has gone to press and the deadline for the second edition is nearing. In the long, desk-cluttered news room telephones ring, typewriters clatter, shirt-sleeved men gripping proof-sheets cluster together in momentary conference or stand, looking preoccupied, bemused or anxious. Half-grown boys dart or dawdle among the desks with more pieces of paper or pots of tea. Now and then someone puts on his hat and goes home. The Night News Editor, a burly Lancashire man, takes another pinch of snuff, stands up from his chair and bawls: "Griff! Look, we're going to be in the —— without that picture of the girl." It doesn't look orderly. But it is.

[1] The known world, at least. Circulation figures for the State-controlled newspapers of Russia and China are unavailable or untrustworthy.

[2] There are nine national dailies: the *Times*, *Daily Telegraph*, *Daily Express*, *Daily Herald*, *Daily Mail*, *Daily Worker*, *News Chronicle*, *Daily Sketch*, *Daily Mirror*—with a combined circulation of nearly 16 million; 10 Sunday papers: *Observer*, *Sunday Times*, *News of the World*, *The People*, *Reynolds News*, *Sunday Dispatch*, *Sunday Express*, *Sunday Graphic*, *Sunday Pictorial*, *Empire News*—with a combined circulation of nearly 30 million.

All the national dailies are morning papers, and the task of getting out an edition is much the same for all of them, quality papers and popular journals alike. A national paper gets its news from two main sources: the news agencies and its own reporters, based on London but sent anywhere in the country (and sometimes abroad) to cover important events. The paper also has a staff of specialists who report and comment on their particular fields of news—political, diplomatic and industrial correspondents, sports writers, theatre and film critics, etc.

The key man in the job of collecting the day's news is the news editor. From his list of forthcoming events he knows in advance what some of the news will be: the opening of Parliament, a trial at the Old Bailey, the Oxford and Cambridge boat race; and he decides which of yesterday's news stories are still "alive" and need following up. He sends reporters out to cover these stories. But all during the day fresh news is breaking; the news editor sends out more reporters, or men who have finished their first assignment, or a man from the provincial office nearest the scene.

About five o'clock there is an editorial conference in the editor's office, to plan the paper. The editor presides, and the various departmental editors—news, foreign, sports, City—report the day's news, actual and expected, in their respective fields. The editor has already seen the "dummy" for tomorrow's paper, in which the advertising manager has sketched in the size and positions of the advertisements, and he has already planned with the features editor what space will be given to the features. The news must be packed into the space remaining, and the conference discusses, in a general way, which news items should be played up and how much space they should have. No hard-and-fast decisions can be made yet.

In the meantime, news is flowing in from agencies, correspondents and reporters. Some of it goes directly to the foreign, City and sports editors; all the rest is handled by the chief sub-editor and his staff. The chief sub-editor, who usually has one or more "copy-tasters" helping him, winnows the grain from the chaff (each newspaper has its own rule of thumb that decides which is which) and marks on each acceptable item how much space he thinks it is worth. These items are then passed to the sub-editors, who cut or rewrite them to the required length, sometimes add explanatory details, fit an appropriate headline and send the copy to the chief sub-editor. When he has passed it, it goes to the composing room.

There it is set by a linotype machine into solid lines of metal type which are built up into columns. Proofs are pulled and sent to various people: proof-readers, "correctors of the Press" (their job is to catch mistakes of fact), a legal expert who watches for libellous statements, the editor, the chief sub-editor, the news editor, the leader writer, etc. More material is set up than can be used, and at this point a further weeding-out takes place. The rest goes to the "stone" (a special table that was once made of stone but is now metal) where the columns of news are fitted into pages. Since other material—advertisements, pictures, cartoons, leaders, features—also has to be fitted in, the make-up of these pages is like putting together a complicated jig-saw puzzle. Each page must fit exactly, so at this point, if a news item takes up too much space and cannot be condensed further, it must be dropped and a shorter item substituted. Since each page has its own deadline (an exact time, with only a few minutes' grace, when the page must leave the composing room for the foundry if the edition is to catch the train) these last-minute decisions must often be made in great haste.

The paper then "goes to press"—i.e., the editorial staff are through with that edition, and the production staff take over. A papier-mâché impression is taken of the flat metal page and bent into a semicircle. From these papier-mâché mats curved metal stereotypes are cast and then clamped in pairs around the rollers of the press. The finished papers emerge from the press automatically cut, folded and counted into quires (25 pages). They are carried on conveyors into the despatch room, where they are wrapped in bundles and taken by vans to the railway station.

As each edition goes to press, work begins on the next. As the news changes or develops during the night, unimportant items are shifted to back pages or dropped. Between the first and the last edition the main news page may be completely re-made, and the final edition often bears very little resemblance to the paper the editorial conference were talking about that afternoon. When the presses stop, in the small hours of the morning, the next day's news has already begun to come in. In a few more hours the morning staff comes to work and the whole thing begins again.

All newspapers are peculiar, but the *Mirror* is more peculiar than others. It actually prides itself on being a sensational tabloid. The word "tabloid" was originally and still is used as a trademark in the drug business by Burroughs Wellcome & Co., and was apparently first applied by Northcliffe to news presented in concentrated or compressed form. The word has got away from its copyright owners and also from Northcliffe, and now generally refers to newspapers smaller than the usual size, and has also taken on a derogatory tinge: "tabloid" is the modern equivalent of the old "yellow journal". And "sensational" is an epithet which the quality Press considers almost but not quite as bad as "irresponsible". Nevertheless, the *Mirror* doesn't mind being typed as a sensational tabloid. It likes its size, it believes the best news is compressed news, and it frankly enjoys being sensational. So do its 14·75 million readers.[1]

The *Mirror's* page measures $14\frac{2}{3} \times 11\frac{3}{4}$ inches, about half the size of the "standard" newspaper. Each page theoretically contains seven narrow columns, but the actual make-up of every page runs riot over these boundaries in a jig-saw of headlines, cartoons, pictures, advertisements and editorial "boxes" (rectangular blocks of type bordered by heavy black lines). At first sight, and until the reader is used to it, the effect

[1] A paper's "readership" is always put at a much higher figure than its paid circulation. The *Mirror's* circulation is something under 5 million, but its *readership*, according to the 1956 Readership Survey of the Institute of Practitioners in Advertising, is 14·75 million, or 40% of British adults. Next biggest: the *Daily Express*, with 12·6 million, or 34%.

is one of tightly packed confusion. But *Mirror* readers soon do get used to it, and learn to find their way around in the smeary jungle of the paper's 24 pages.

The first page is a show-window, to catch the eye. It always has a big black headline, often in letters two inches high, and almost always an arresting photograph, taking up half the page for more. Occasionally, when the *Mirror* has something particularly emphatic to say, it drops the picture and spreads an editorial, in heavy type, all over the front page. The other most important pages, by *Mirror* formula, are the two in the centre (the "centre spread"), where the *Mirror* usually puts on its act for the day: the exposure of a scandal, pictures of a royal tour, a striking news photograph of a disaster, a sentimental story or picture of an animal or a baby. Each of the *Mirror's* regular features—the leader, Vicky's cartoon, "Cassandra's" and Richard Crossman's columns, The Old Codgers' answers to correspondents, the strip cartoons, etc.—has its regular position in the paper, which the readers soon learn. News stories of "human interest" are played up; other news is compressed to a paragraph or two. The *Mirror* avoids run-overs (stories that run over into a following page) except when it feels it simply must give its readers all the warm, grisly, intimate details. World news is usually tucked in, in small type, on the back page.

It might surprise people who never read the *Mirror* to discover that most of the actual reporting in the paper is quiet, factual and unsensational. The swaggering style, the shouted phrase is reserved for some of the *Mirror's* features and particularly for the belligerent voice of the paper itself, in headlines and leaders. The characteristic *Mirror* headline reads like a slogan chalked on a brick wall:

SACK THE LOT

or

EDEN IS A FLOP

or

HURRY UP, MARGARET

A classic example was the *Mirror's* wartime headline about the evacuation of the British Army from Dunkirk:

BLOODY
MARVELLOUS

As all its readers know, the *Mirror* has a warm and sentimental heart, with an especially soft spot for young lovers, babies and the right kind of animals (cats, dogs and horses)—in ascending order of softness. On October 23, 1956 the *Mirror's* front page carried the headline Crisis in Poland: REDS SEND CRUISERS. But more than half the page was taken up by a photograph of a girl caressing a dog, with this story underneath:

"Schoolgirl Gillian Pepler, 15, gave her fox terrier pal a hug at her home last night (above). And gently the terrier gave her a 'kiss'.

"But it wasn't always like that. For fifteen months the terrier—a stray—ran wild. All through last winter he slept on doorsteps or on the common at Wimbledon.

"He SNARLED at people who tried to feed him, SNAPPED when police went too near, RAN when inspectors from the R.S.P.C.A. tried to help him.

"Everybody called him The Tramp. No one, it seemed, could make friends with him. And he grew wild and spiteful.

"Then along came Gillian. . . .

"She was walking across the common with her own dog, Brandy, a mongrel, when The Tramp appeared.

"Gillian tried to be friendly, but The Tramp kept his distance.

"Young Gillian saw The Tramp often after that, and threw him food.

"*Slowly she won his friendship.*

"Then one day the terrier followed Gillian home to Merton Hall Road, Wimbledon.

"He slept in the garden . . . and snarled at anyone who came too close.

"But one night there was a bad thunderstorm.

"Gillian opened the front door, and The Tramp trotted in. He joined mongrel Brandy in front of the fire.

"*Now Gillian has TWO dogs—and The Tramp has found a home.*"

The *Mirror* has a big warm heart; it has a conscience too. It says so itself. In 1956 the *Mirror* declared its social faith: "We believe in ordinary people. So we find in Britain today more reasons for being happy than for being miserable.... We rejoice in the good humour, the fine spirit and the success with which the British people are tackling the problems of modern life. . . . We stand for equal opportunities for all children, good homes and robust health for everyone, a high standard of living for all. And we challenge every vested interest, whatever its political colour, that obstructs the realisation of that ideal. . . . So we strive to smash every artificial barrier to full expression of the moral qualities of the British people at home and in the Commonwealth. That is the faith that defines our daily purpose."

The *Mirror* itself seems to be proud of the fact that nearly a third of its readers do not know which party the *Mirror* supports—a striking commentary on the intelligence of its audience. Fifty-five per cent, however, have the right answer: the *Mirror* is pro-Labour. It has to be, if it wants to be in tune with its readers, who generally vote that way. But the *Mirror* makes a great play of not being tied to the Labour Party, as the *Daily Herald* is, and occasionally takes a fall out of one of Labour's leaders or even the Party management.

The *Mirror* believes that it wields great political power; in fact, it considers itself the greatest political power in Britain. The paper takes a large share of the credit for Labour's post-war victory in 1945; in subsequent elections won by the Conservatives the *Mirror* feels that it was instrumental in whittling down the size of the majority ("Keep the Tories Tame"). Some of the Press tends to agree with the *Mirror's* estimate of itself. The weekly *Truth* has testified: "The *Daily Mirror* prints less political news than any other paper, but its political influence is very great. This is because it specialises in political campaigns, argued in terms that only the educationally under-privileged would understand or even believe."

Who are the *Mirror's* readers? In the words of a *Mirror* advertisement, they are "working class mostly. . . . They own more than half the television sets in the country. They are buying washing machines, radiograms, refrigerators and even cars. . . . Yes, they are the people with money to spend these days. . . . They are the mass market, old boy. The only market worth advertising to in these days." The *Mirror's* relations with its readers are as close and cosy as the paper can make them. Instead of trying to tell them what they ought to do or ought to think, it tells them how they feel and encourages them in the feeling.

Sometimes, when the *Mirror* is not quite sure where its readers stand, it asks them—about Princess Margaret and Captain Townsend, for example. After the hanging of Ruth Ellis (a woman who had shot an ex-lover as he came out of a Hampstead pub) the *Mirror* asked its readers how they felt about capital punishment, and nodded approvingly when they voted nearly two to one against it. All popular newspapers are continually trying to find out more about their readers and what they like and dislike; the *Mirror* believes it knows more on this subject than any other paper. For one thing, *Mirror* readers form a more homogeneous group than the readers of the *Express*, for instance, or even the *News of the World*.

The *Mirror's* readers share the same lack of interest in highbrow subjects, the same level of education, much the same prejudices and hopes. What these people want from their paper is a bit of fun, a bit of colour, a bit of news (lots of sports news and some sex and crime, but go easy on the foreign stuff and Parliament) and strip cartoons and maybe a feature or two—just enough to keep them pleasantly occupied for six minutes on the bus or the Tube or the train on their way to the job in the morning. Six minutes a day: that is the average reading time, according to the *Mirror's* own findings.

But in that daily six minutes the *Mirror* tells them quite a lot: that they live in an amazingly exciting but very down-to-earth sort of world, where lightning strikes boy-and-girl lovers, men commit murder for other men's wives, where warmongers with an H-bomb or uncontrolled automation or the selfish plans of power-hungry men may be the end of us—but not if we keep our wits about us and remember that we have the guts and the brains (and the mass power) to keep all such villains and man-made catastrophes under control. Meantime, there is a never-ending parade of ludicrous, pathetic, heart-warming and appetising people and events: pretty girls in bathing suits and strip cartoons, fat men asleep, animals that look human and humans that look like animals, children that are lost and found again, wives who know what to do when their husbands come home late, drunk and disorderly—an inexhaustible cornucopia pouring out the fascinating minutiae of everyday life.

As a Features Editor of the *Mirror* once said: "What was the use of worrying readers about obscure revolutions in Bolivia if they could not sleep at night through indigestion? Was a pregnant woman, whose husband could not possibly afford her fourth child, interested in a Parliamentary debate on foreign affairs which would obviously result in nothing at all? What was the point of publishing pompous articles by avaricious big-wigs when figures proved that nobody would read them? Did newspapers really care what their customers read, or didn't they know how to find out? . . . Had it ever occurred to Fleet Street that people didn't want to read anything at all?"

If a newspaper's personality is pontifical and public, like the *Times*' or the *Daily Telegraph's*, it will tell its readers what it considers they *ought* to know about; it will give them all the details it can of that obscure revolution in Bolivia, regardless of whether or not they have indigestion and cannot sleep. If, on the other hand, a paper's personality is private and plebeian, like the *Mirror's*, it will mainly report the news it thinks its readers would *like* to know about; it may also give them the latest tips on indigestion.

Non-readers of the *Mirror* are likely to make the mistake of thinking that the *Mirror* has abandoned all pretence of being a newspaper in the old-fashioned sense, and has become in fact nothing but a daily magazine of entertaining features. This is not the case, however. When the Royal Commission on the Press made an analysis of three papers (the *Times*, *Daily Mail* and *Daily Mirror*) for the three years 1927, 1937 and 1947, it found that "in the *Daily Mirror* news steadily increased in importance between 1927 and 1947 while pictures steadily declined. Features did not change very much. Strip and comic cartoons increased very greatly. . . . In the allocation of editorial space there was considerably more resemblance between the three newspapers in 1947 than in the earlier years."

The *Mirror* has no definite programme but it knows which way it's heading: it's going the way "the people" are going. Sideways? Backwards? Round and round? No, sir—forward! The *Mirror* is in step with the working class; it's a class paper first, last and all the time. The people should have better pay, better food, better houses, more fun, more colour in their lives, more and better education, more and better TV, cars instead of motor bikes, butter instead of marge. There are more of them than anybody and they have more votes: all they have to do is get together and they are bound to get what they want. They should be running the country instead of the Tories, and they will, as sure as God made little apples. And this time they will run it for keeps. They are on the march, says the *Mirror*, in their slow British way (but getting faster now) and they will get there; in larger and larger numbers they are getting there already—to Fleet Street, to the City, into Parliament, into industry.

The old Tory England has gone for ever; the old Liberal middle-class England is as good as dead. The new England will be the people's country, the land of the *Mirror* reader. That is the *Mirror's* real news.

The Men behind the Mirror

A newspaper is first and foremost a personality, but a newspaper is produced by its staff. More than 3,000 people are regularly employed by the *Mirror*, of whom about 300 do the actual reporting, writing and editing. Two men head the complex hierarchy of the paper: Cecil Harmsworth King and Hugh Cudlipp.

Cecil King, as Chairman of the Daily Mirror Newspapers Ltd. and of the Sunday Pictorial Newspapers Ltd., is the real boss. In some ways he is the biggest man in Fleet Street, and knows it. His slightly older cousin Esmond, the second Lord Rothermere, inheritor of the title and of Northcliffe's *Daily Mail*, and for years regarded as an adequate if lesser chip off the old Harmsworth block, has been increasingly diminished by the rise of Cecil King. Harmsworth is King's middle name, and Harmsworth is his nature.

Cecil King is a big man: 6 ft. 4 and well over 200 pounds, running to fat; though he is a hard worker, he works sitting down. His thinning hair is blond but at 56 is greying. If it were not for his aggressive Harmsworth nose and the stubborn set of his lips, he would look not unlike a large, placidly intelligent baby. His expression, sometimes ironical, sometimes peevishly impatient, usually seems to hint a controlled, mildly amused exasperation. In a relaxed mood he can give an impression of rumpled benevolence, but under the benevolence there is something sharp and watchful, as if the clock that measures his valuable time were never quite out of his sight. His staff regard him as shy, and consider him a hard man to talk to. At company parties he is notorious for his inability to put people at their ease. He is a tycoon and a cold one, still a little awkward in the part.

His background and education, as well as his nature, set him apart from his fellows on the *Mirror*. His father, Sir Lucas King, was a civil servant in India, his mother, a Harmsworth, a sister of Northcliffe and Rothermere, was a rich woman. Cecil King was educated at Winchester and Christ Church, Oxford. He took a Second Class in History there in 1920. One of his contemporaries at Christ Church (for a year) was Henry R. Luce, founder and Editor-in-chief of Time Inc., for whom King expresses the kindly contempt of one successful man for another.

When Rothermere sold his controlling interest in the *Mirror* in 1936, Cecil King became the power behind the scenes. And there he was content to remain till 1951, when Bartholomew resigned from the post of Chairman and he took it for himself. Years of hard and quiet work had taught him the newspaper business inside and out; he knew more about running a popular newspaper than either his uncle or his cousin.

A lonely man who has few friends and interests outside his work, he has even taken on some of the characteristics of his paper's personality, and they sit rather oddly on him. He is not naturally sentimental, particularly not about children, but the *Mirror* is, so King talks about them as if he were too. The *Mirror* does not believe in being cynical; neither does King. (A fellow-journalist has said of him that *tactically* he is not cynical, *strategically* he is.) One of his few close friends is Malcolm Muggeridge, editor of *Punch*, who charmed him, early in their acquaintance, by telling him the story of the two tramps who were discussing women; one admitted that he would rather dream of a woman than have one, "because you meet a better class of woman that way". Muggeridge said the *Mirror* reminded him of that tramp.

King is under no illusions about the quality of tabloid journalism; in a letter to Churchill during the war he described it as "a raw, crude medium but very typical of its day". Perhaps it is partly a feeling of defensiveness on his part that has resulted in the extent and variety of the *Mirror's* "prestige advertising"—ventures that are not profitable in themselves but are intended to reflect credit on the paper and build up public goodwill for it. The *Mirror* puts on an annual show of pictures by children, and sends it on tour through Britain, Europe and America; it also sponsors a children's orchestra, which fills the Albert Hall when it gives its annual concert in London. Two or three times a year the *Mirror* puts out a well-produced, well-written pamphlet on some current problem (e.g., Anglo-American relations, defence, education, the law courts). The furthest-fetched piece of prestige advertising was *The London Magazine*, a literary monthly which the *Mirror* supported until King decided that it wasn't worth it.

King's first concern, as the man in charge of the *Mirror's* destinies, is not so much its policies as its continued commercial success. His job is to expand and secure the *Mirror's* position in every possible way. For weeks at a time he is off on business trips—to Canada, where his Anglo-Canadian Pulp and Paper Mills have doubled their production since 1934; to Australia, where the *Mirror* owns a weekly (*Australasian Post*) and has an interest in radio stations; to West Africa, where the *Mirror* owns six dailies; to Manchester, where the *Mirror's* northern edition is now printed, and Glasgow, where it recently bought two Kemsley papers.

One thing that King no longer has to worry about is the *Mirror's* survival. But he is sorry (or says he is) for some of the *Mirror's* competitors, and deplores the sad probability that they will be driven to the wall. "Greedy labour unions and inept management are driving other newspapers out of business," he says. "I hope they don't, really, because I like to see variety. But one thing I know. The *Mirror* will flourish." King is naturally more interested in cultivating the growth of the *Mirror* and its enterprises than he is in the care and feeding of the Labour Party. "The *Mirror* is leftish, of course," he says, "but we've been moving right for the past two years. That's because the country has been moving right. The standard of living is higher, and the worker now likes to consider himself middle-class."

While King's job as Chairman is to take the long view, like a chief of staff working out the strategy for a whole campaign, he leaves the day-to-day, week-to-week tactics of the *Mirror* to his Editorial Director, Hugh Cudlipp. Cudlipp is a very pure example of the new kind of editor evolved by mass-circulation journalism. The type has been described by the Royal Commission on the Press:

> We have been told that as a result of the emergence of big financial corporations in the newspaper industry and the consequent influence of commercial considerations upon the conduct of the newspapers which they own, the authority and the status of the editor have declined. This complaint appears to us to be misconceived. The truth is, not so much that the status of editors has declined, as that a new type of paper has been created which calls for a new kind of editor. A popular paper appealing to a mass readership has no use for a Delane or a C. P. Scott. Its character and success depend on something quite other than the authoritative discussion of public affairs: they depend on the power to interest and entertain a wide variety of readers whose concern with politics as such is limited and intermittent.
>
> If an editor's main business is to increase the mass-circulation of a paper which is not sold and read mainly for its views, he will have a great many things to think about besides the formation of public opinion—so many that he cannot give to public affairs in their higher aspects the same degree of close attention which the older type of editor gave. The natural consequence is that he ceases to wield the chief influence on that side; he may even count for less there than some of his colleagues, and must usually count for far less than the chief proprietor. In short, the editor of a popular paper rarely has or can have the influence on policy exercised by the editor of a quality paper.

While in general this description of an editor fits Cudlipp's function, it does not, in certain particulars, fit him. Belligerent and quick-tempered, with the assured arrogance of earned and precocious success, he would never submit now (though earlier in his career he might have endured it) to a subordinate position in which he merely carried out orders. Both he and King serve the same demanding master, the *Mirror*, and each of them has to furnish the supply for different demands. King is the boss; he can say No to Cudlipp; but if he said No too often, Cudlipp would leave.

Hugh Cudlipp might have been a brilliant politician. He has the voice for it, the presence, the orator's hunched and brooding look. A chunky man of medium height, with a big brow emphasised by the retreating line of his curly hair, and deep-sunk, darting eyes, he has the cultivated bluffness and shrewd frankness of a veteran hail-fellow. He is a conversational welterweight, fast on his feet, tireless, and a master of the counterpunch. In an energetic profession, his energy is already legendary. It would be hard to imagine him in even momentary despair, or more than momentarily undecided. He has the engaging confidence—it would be too much to call it charm—of a man who knows where he has been and thinks he knows where he is going. He is good company and no one ever found him hard to talk to. He is not an intellectual, though he knows how to use intellectuals in his business, but a man of action, an executive.

Hugh Cudlipp is the youngest of three brothers, born in a working-class household in Cardiff, South Wales. His father was a commercial traveller in groceries. The Cudlipp boys were all outstandingly bright, outstandingly ambitious. All of them went into journalism, at the bottom, and all got to the top: Percy, now 50, as editor of the *Daily Herald*, official paper of the Labour Party (he resigned in 1954 and now edits the weekly *New Scientist*; Reginald, as editor of *News of the World*, the weekly crime-and-scandal sheet which is avidly read by nearly 20 million Britishers, from dukes to dustmen; Hugh to the highest eminence of all. He joined the *Mirror* in 1935, in answer to an advertisement: "WANTED: Bright Features sub. able to take charge." He got the job, and took charge of the *Mirror's* features during the tabloid revolution.

Cudlipp flung himself into that revolution with a whole heart and an undivided, ambitious mind. He saw what this kind of sensational journalism might accomplish—or at least what audience it could catch. In his book on the *Mirror*, *Publish and Be Damned!*, he tells about those days: "Behind the barking and the tinsel, however, was a closely reasoned scheme. The plan which these young men evolved was simply this—to get under the readers' skin and to stay there. They were all, in their way, lay psychologists. Most of them had come from working-class or middle-class families in the provinces; they really knew and had personally experienced the aspirations and setbacks, the joys and the heartaches of thc millions of ordinary people whom they set out to entertain and instruct. The down-to-earth feature pages became more and more like a letter home to the family, and that was their secret."

In 1937 Cudlipp was made Editor of the *Sunday Pictorial*. He was then 24, the youngest editor in Fleet Street. When he and Bartholomew had a row and Cudlipp resigned, Beaverbrook immediately hired him and made him managing editor of the *Sunday Express*. But Beaverbrook and his policies were not really to Cudlipp's liking, and when, two years later, Bartholomew was out and the road was clear again, Cudlipp went happily home to the *Mirror*.

Although the *Mirror* and the other papers under his direction all have their own editors, Cudlipp's restless spirit moves him constantly to take a direct hand in their editorial affairs, especially in the *Mirror's*. Whenever the front page really lets out a roar (*Princess Margaret*—THIS CRUEL PLAN MUST BE EXPOSED or COME ON MARGARET! OR IS SHE SAD?) or the leader pounds the table harder than usual ("*We can all get on together. . . . Let's invite the Russian leaders to Britain. . . .* Why not invite them—NOW? We have nothing to lose but our icicles"), or the *Mirror* starts a new crusade (almost invariably anti-Tory, anti-Army or anti-upper-class), the chances are ten to one that Hugh Cudlipp is speaking or has thought it up or is directly concerned in it. He too goes on business trips, sometimes to far Australia, and takes week-ends on his motor-boat on the Thames; but he is seldom out of touch, and when the *Mirror* shoots it is usually his finger on the trigger.

As the *Mirror's* chief tactician, Cudlipp decides the direction and extent of the *Mirror's* daily attack. His job is to get the paper talked about, to keep it brash and surprising, to invent new stunts and eye-catching campaigns. The scope and violence of these tactics are only limited—but they are limited—by the necessity of preserving and developing the *Mirror's* personality, which is its principal weapon.

King and Cudlipp are the two men who, in their different ways, direct the *Mirror's* course; but there are others who make the paper what it is. First, the star turns. The *Mirror's* most famous property, almost its trademark, is the best-known strip cartoon in Britain, "Jane". Jane has been going since pre-war days (December, 1932), and has long outlasted her original creator; she is now the work of an anonymous team. Jane is a pretty girl whose endless and endlessly pointless adventures with men show her in various stages of alluring undress, but never quite naked.

There was one exception, during the dark days of the war, and the great occasion was reported by an American Forces paper in the Far East, under the headline JANE GIVES ALL: "Well, sirs, you can go home now. Right smack out of the blue and with no one even threatening her, Jane peeled a week ago. The British 36th Division immediately gained six miles and the British attacked in the Arakan. Maybe we Americans ought to have Jane too." The *Mirror* runs a daily page of strip cartoons, but Jane always has a place to herself on another page.

Next to Jane in order of tradition and probably more popular with *Mirror* readers is the letter-answering department, Live Letters, "conducted by the Old Codgers". This is a kind of two-way chat between the *Mirror* and its readers; it also answers questions, gives a "thought for the day", and once a week runs a list of people (initials or first names only) who are ill, bereaved or in trouble, and asks *Mirror* readers to pray for them. Samples:

Mrs. W. Hunt wrote indignantly about the bad manners of tourists in front of Buckingham Palace, especially those who made fun of the sentries. The Old Codgers replied sympathetically: "If the sentries aren't ringed with grinning oafs, they have so-called 'starlets' flaunting past them, with photographers in attendance. We've often wondered what a Palace sentry really thinks of the lot of 'em, and if one of them cares to tell us we'll gladly print it."

"Alma" asked why a little lace mat is called a doily. "Takes its name from a firm of London linen drapers which existed from the time of Queen Anne until about 1850."

"Pedestrian" felt that traffic accidents would be halved if photographs of the victims were shown to all drivers. The Old Codgers did not agree: "American papers habitually print gruesome smash pictures, and look at THEIR road accidents."

TODAY'S THOUGHT: "As long as I have a want, I have a reason for living. Satisfaction is death.—Bernard Shaw."

The best if not the most popular of the *Mirror's* star turns is "Cassandra's" column. "Cassandra's" identity is no secret: his picture appears at the top of his column, and all Fleet Street, at least, knows his name—William Neil Connor. There is no other columnist in Britain like Cassandra. A rough equivalent (but a very rough equivalent) in the United States is Westbrook Pegler, the syndicated Hearst columnist. But Pegler is a professionally angry reactionary, while Cassandra is a professionally rude liberal. Both men have exploited the kind of public outspokenness that appeals mightily to more timid and less eloquent private citizens—"in the only profession", according to Hugh Cudlipp, "where big-scale, incessant rudeness (skilfully written) is highly paid".

Connor joined the *Mirror* in 1935, on the same day Cudlipp did. He had already learned how to write arresting copy in the London branch of J. Walter Thompson, the U.S. advertising agency. On the *Mirror* he started on the Old Codgers' homely correspondence section, graduated from that to the Cassandra column, which he soon made over into his own plump, dour, bespectacled image. The *Mirror* gave him his head. An individualist, humanitarian and political independent, he can be counted on to disagree with almost anybody about almost anything. He has said in his column that his favourite paper (he reads them all, including the *Mirror*) is the *Manchester Guardian*. Cassandra's opinions are stoutly held and violently expressed; he sometimes overbids a weak hand but he always slaps his cards down with gusto.

Here is his comment on a Roman Catholic attempt to distinguish between sinful and non-sinful kisses: "In a world crammed with starving humanity, a world teetering on self-annihilation with hydrogen bombs, these dead theologians who have never smelt the blossom in May or seen the inviting leeward side of a haystack have to come out with this desiccated humbug." On American motor cars: "One of those great landship American cars that from the back looks like a shark with chromium-plated fins, and from the front looks like an angry mouth-organ." He didn't like the touring American entertainer Liberace, and said so. Some of his remarks reached the U.S. Press and drew angry letters from Liberace fans, whereupon Cassandra hit him again—and was sued for libel, no new experience for Cassandra.

His hammering style hits off echoes that are sometimes Carlylean, sometimes Kiplingesque. He can be as eloquent as P. G. Wodehouse and is always as readable as Macaulay:

> One of these unfine days I shall find myself, I suppose, in a celestial—or more likely hellish—waiting-room preparing myself for an interview with St. Peter—or the Prince of Darkness.
>
> And then either His Reverence or His Irreverence will say to me: "Now how did you spend your time on earth?"
>
> "Well, your Eminence—or your Lowness," I shall say, "I wrote a great deal of nonsense in my time, but I had a fine time doing it. I saw a lot of things and I met great numbers of people. I knew plenty of crooks (this will go down well

with the Prince of Darkness) and I knew at least one eminently good man (this may curry favour with St. Peter but I doubt it).

"I witnessed bits of five wars, saw Vesuvius blow up, swam the Thames at Shadwell, saved Deal Gasworks from the Royal Artillery—a complicated yarn this, but I'll tell you about it one day—made a forty-two-egg omelette next to the leaning tower of Pisa, and heard Toscanini give his first concert after Mussolini at the Scala, Milan. I can also grow tomatoes and I understand the minds of cats perfectly." . . .

In June, 1940, in response to an appeal by General Sir Hubert Gough, I, with thousands of other people, gave or lent binoculars to His Majesty's Government. We were glad to do so.

In 1946 some of the donors wrote to the Government asking if they could either have their glasses back or, maybe, buy them back at a reasonable price, as they surmised that there might be a surplus.

They were either ignored or given the official brush-off.

What happened to those binoculars? Some were destroyed. But thousands of pairs were undoubtedly gratefully looted.

The rest? Well, the Select Committee on Estimates has just uncovered the fact that the Government has hoarded 24,000 prismatic binoculars (excluding war reserves) and has enough of them at present consumption rates to last for the next thirty-four years.

Dear Prime Minister, Dear Chancellor of the Exchequer, Dear Secretary of State for War, Dear Secretary of State for Air, Dear First Lord of the Admiralty, may we have our binoculars back, please?

Or maybe you could sell us, at a cheap rate, one of those 346,568 chairs that the Army holds in peacetime reserve for some spectacular wartime emergency in which a third of a million men may suddenly be ordered to sit down.

Or one of the 7,000 "Heavy Duty Bicycles" that the Army

hangs on to for a nameless day out on the roads after the nuclear war has begun.

Or perhaps we might have a free issue of blanco—just one packet out of the scores of tons held in reserve that will last the Army for the next ten years.

I can think of nothing better than to await the Hydrogen Bomb, blancoed up to the eyebrows, seated on Army Chair No. 346,568, scanning the future with a surplus pair of binoculars earmarked for the war of 1991, with a heavy duty bicycle drawn up alongside so as to be able to get the hell out of it.

Hugh Cudlipp has said of him: "Cassandra disagrees with almost everything the *Mirror* stands for. He is armed with intolerance, bigotry, and irascibility. But the *Mirror* would be a duller place without him." It certainly would. Duller, and worse.

Another star turn, who in order of popularity should rank with or perhaps above Cassandra, is the *Mirror's* chief sports writer, Peter Wilson, billed as "the man they can't gag". One of the few Old School Tie boys (Harrow) on the *Mirror*, Wilson looks as jovial as Connor looks glum. Tall, burly, red-haired, with slightly pop eyes and sweeping moustaches, he resembles a polo-playing cavalry officer gone a bit paunchy. A veteran sports writer, he roams the world and the whole field of sport, covering pretty much what he wants to. Since four of the Mirror's 24 pages are regularly filled with news of sport, the job of star performer in this department is one of the best-paid and most-sought-after berths in Fleet Street.

Richard Howard Stafford Crossman, who began writing a three-times-a-week column for the *Mirror* in September, 1955, was a new departure for the *Mirror*—an admitted intellectual. If Cassandra can be compared with Pegler, Crossman might be likened to Walter Lippmann. But Crossman is much less a pundit than a propagandist. An Oxford man and formerly a don at New College, Crossman has the teacher's zeal to instruct, and he has always pined for bigger and bigger classes. In the *Mirror's* audience, he has the biggest yet—if they will listen. A Member of Parliament since 1945, he is a left-wing member of the Labour Party's executive council. Personable, articulate, friendly and frank, Crossman is an enthusiast who has notably failed to rouse the enthusiasm of his fellow-Britons. This coolness may be partly explained by the deep distrust felt by the British for intellectuals in general as "unsound" or "too clever by half".

Crossman's assignment on the *Mirror* is to explain in simplified language which millions of readers can understand what is going on in domestic and foreign politics. Officially, he does not speak for the *Mirror*, any more than Cassandra does, but of course neither he nor Cassandra would last long if the *Mirror* found their views completely unsympathetic: i.e., if the majority of *Mirror* readers found them unreadable or turned against them.

Cassandra and Crossman's column are at least partly informative and thought-provoking, but many of the *Mirror's* features are not even intended to be anything but entertaining. The most entertaining of the lot is Donald Zec's page of interviews with movie stars. The quizzical dialogue in which he reports a conversation between himself and some hen-brained beauty of the screen is often extremely funny.

Noel Whitcomb, who also writes gossip about notorieties, is a dapper, lively little extravert who gives the impression of being overdressed for a party and quite amused by his costume. He has curly blond hair and the crinkled, prematurely aged face of a boy who has been eavesdropping on his elders for years and now knows more than they think. When he makes the kind of mistake to which knowing journalists are liable, such as referring airily to "Dostoyevsky's great novel, *War and Peace*", it puts him only momentarily out of countenance. He has the gift of gab, like all the feature writers on the *Mirror*; once you read his first sentence, you'll probably be lured on to the end.

The *Mirror's* "sob sister", one of the best in the business, is

Mary Brown, a small, red-haired, middle-aged woman with a sad, kind face. She has never worked on any other paper. After the war, alarmed by the general let-down in manners and morals, she wrote an article on "Responsibility", and a friend persuaded her to send it to the *Mirror*. That got her a job. Mary Brown gives advice to the love-lorn, to anxious parents, to uncertain adolescents and to troubled husbands or wives—though she always tries to get these last to take their case to the Marriage Guidance Council. She not only answers all her letters personally (about 45 a day) but frequently goes to see the people who write to her, and tries to help them straighten out their problems. Herself the child of a poor family in dockside London who has had her share of hardship and misery, she writes with the conviction and charity of a wise and experienced woman. Here is a sample question-and-answer:

> "Do I marry a girl who has lied to me?" This is the question Tony cannot answer. Writing from Peterborough, he says:
>
> "When I came home from two years' National Service, I heard that my girl Theresa had been seen out with other chaps. When I asked her about it she said it wasn't true.
>
> "Quite unexpectedly, I received proof that it was true. So I tackled her again. Then she broke down and cried bitterly.
>
> "She said it was true, but she was afraid to tell me. She said she loved me and had never done anything wrong, and these boys meant nothing to her.
>
> "What I don't understand is—if she didn't care about them, why did she go out with them? And why did she tell me lies?
>
> "I'm terribly worried about all this because we planned to get married at Christmas, when she's nineteen. I love my girl very much, but I keep wondering—will it work out?
>
> "I know I must make my own decision, but I'd like your views."

Why did Theresa go out with other boys? Two years is a long time for a very young girl to be alone. The girls she works with would talk about the pictures and dances they had been to with their boy friends. Tony expected Theresa to sit at home every night and like it.

I say she did no wrong by accepting occasional invitations, and the fact that she went out with "boys" and not one boy should have reassured Tony. All she wanted was an escort.

But she certainly was foolish not to write and tell Tony at the time. And she wronged herself and him by lying to him when he came home.

But Tony is not blameless. He admits Theresa was "afraid" to tell him the truth. This indicates that he is not a very easy person to tell things to.

And I think now he might put himself in his girl's place and imagine how he would have felt if she were so touchy, jealous and possessive that he was afraid to be frank with her.

He must not marry Theresa until he can trust her. Without trust he will be forever suspecting. And when you get like that, you can always read guilt into the other person's most innocent words and actions. . . .

Love that cannot stand the test of two years' separation (punctuated by a fair amount of leave) will certainly not last a lifetime.

And it is better to have this fact proved for you sooner than later.

Unless Cassandra feels like talking about one, as occasionally he does, the *Mirror* does not review books, nor plays, music or art, because its readers do not read books, nor go to the theatre, nor the concert hall, nor the art galleries. But they all have television sets, or mostly, so the *Mirror* runs a daily list of TV programmes and comment. And they go to the cinema, so once a week Reg Whitley tells them which shows they'll like.

He knows, because they're the ones he likes himself, and he has unerring common taste. If he were a Hollywood director he could save—and make—his company a lot of money.

The writers form the visible part of the *Mirror*, but most of the iceberg is below the surface. As Fleet Street knows, they are not in any sense submerged characters. One of the most important is Donald Zec's brother Philip, who used to be the *Mirror's* political cartoonist and is now a director.[1] One of his jobs is to ride herd on the seven daily strip cartoons, each of which is consciously fashioned to appeal to different tastes or to a different group of readers.

These picture stories are literally endless, and Zec must keep each of them up to the mark, in character and in contrast. Some of the difficulties he has to deal with are psychological, almost psychiatric. Once, when he and the cartoonist were discussing the next episode for Belinda (a sentimentally appealing teen-age girl who always triumphs over misfortune), they hit on a situation which required that Belinda should be given a certain sum of money. Perhaps £200? Thinking it over, Zec decided that £200 was far too much, an astronomical figure in the economy of *Mirror* readers—besides, Belinda was just a little girl. The cartoonist looked at him and said, "Why, you mean bastard!"

Every newspaper is organised in such a way that everyone on its staff is accountable to someone else slightly above him in the organisation. In theory (and in legal liability) this would put the Editor at the top, but the *Mirror* does not work that way in practice. The actual editorial boss is Cudlipp, and in his régime the job of Editor is largely supervisory. The Editor, Jack Nener, is an old-fashioned newspaper man, bluff, gregarious, full of brag and bluster, the commoner oaths and stories of his profession. A fine figure of a middle-aged man, with a high complexion, a small moustache slightly darker than the dramatic white tousle of his head, and black-framed spectacles, he is easily recognisable and widely known. He normally keeps

[1] Zec has now left the *Mirror* for the *Daily Herald* and has gone back to cartooning.

daylight office hours; after presiding over the editorial conference at 5.30, at which he criticises yesterday's paper and makes suggestions for tomorrow's, and after reading the first edition, he leaves the office in charge of his deputy, Richard Dinsdale.

Dinsdale is a newspaperman's newspaperman; usually there is one of him in every well-run organisation. He is the kind of quiet person who seems to be everywhere at once, doing everything at once, anticipating the next need, rescuing the latest disaster without hurry or flurry; knowledgeable, reassuring, level-headed. He keeps the list of never-ending things-to-be-done in his head, in orderly file. Well after the first edition has gone to press but while the second is still in the chaos of creation, and having put in a day that most men would consider work enough for two, he goes home, reluctantly. He has done all he could; the rest is up to the night staff.

Whose is the guiding intelligence that shapes each day's paper, decides what to put in, what to leave out, and gets the edition into finished form? No one man. In practice, there is simply not time enough to submit every decision to the top authority; the great mass of detailed daily problems are settled as they arise, right down the editorial line.

No one man, whether he is chairman or editor-in-chief or editor, can control all the details of a great newspaper. The job is too big, and there are too many details. No one man decides exactly which items will be included and which left out, and how every news story is to be handled. The editor and his assistants plan the general lay-out of the paper, what the subject and tone of the leader is to be, and what news items should be played up. But these are tentative decisions, subject to changing circumstances, and in any case the work itself must be done by subordinates.

Before the paper goes to press or he to bed, the editor usually sees proofs of the most important items, but he won't know exactly what's in the paper till he sees it next morning. Though he is legally responsible for every word in it, he may find some surprises—sometimes most disagreeable surprises. In that case, all he can do is give somebody a piece of his mind. Or, if it was a very bad mistake, and he can lay his finger on the guilty party—which is not always easy and often impossible—he can fire him.

What do They Think They're Doing?

It would be a mistake to suppose that King and Cudlipp, both intelligent men, care only for the kind of success that can be measured in advertising revenue, circulation, or an irresponsible influence over a mass of readers. It is a mistake quite often made by the *Mirror's* critics. The charge is too sweeping. King and Cudlipp are conscious of their responsible position; it doesn't scare them; they take pride in it. The Royal Commission on the Press, having considered the evidence on this question, decided that "if there is in almost all newspaper ownership some admixture of commercial motives, we believe that it is also true that most newspaper undertakings conceive themselves to be rendering a service to the public. The strength and clarity of this conception vary according to the character of the undertaking, and so do its consequences in the conduct of the paper; but its existence should always be allowed for in discussing either the present or the future of the Press. There is still widespread among Pressmen a sense of vocation; they feel a call, somewhat as sailors feel the call of the sea."

Though Cecil King might not permit himself the metaphor, he would subscribe to the idea: he would say that the *Mirror* is rendering a service to the public. A large part of that service is entertainment; but from King's point of view (and Cudlipp's) the entertainment is the sugar on a very serious and effective pill. Everyone on the *Mirror*, from King to the boy who carries copy, understands that, in some degree. The whole staff knows and likes the *Mirror's* personality, its tone of voice, the kind of news it tells.

Each paper reports its chosen items in its own tone of voice.

The *Mirror's* tone of voice is as unmistakably and self-consciously its own as the *Times's*. Its blatancy is deliberate and has been deliberately cultivated to a point where every seasoned member of the editorial staff knows without being told how the *Mirror* does and does not speak. Revolutionised into a tabloid and relieved of its middle-class concerns and pretences, the *Mirror* found itself—and also found readers by the million. The *Mirror* now believes that its kind of news and its method of reporting are far and away the best for a *modern* newspaper, and will increasingly be so in the future.

Does Cecil King know what he is doing in enabling the *Mirror* to speak with an ever louder voice? Perhaps not even he could answer that question, beyond the firm assertion that the *Mirror* is rendering a public service. But he is obviously doing something else besides that: he would be less or more than human if he weren't aware that he has already beaten Beaverbrook and his cousin Rothermere at their own game, and bids fair to surpass his two uncles, Northcliffe and the first Lord Rothermere.

And Hugh Cudlipp—what does he think he is doing? As he must know himself, he's making the biggest noise on Fleet Street. If he were to put it on a postcard, perhaps the message would read like this: "Having wonderful time. Don't you wish you were here?"

As for the writers and editors, the men who get out the paper—do they ever stop to consider what they are up to? What have they got up their sleeves? Most of them have nothing whatever up their sleeves but a good right arm: they work hard at a job which they take pride and pleasure in doing well. Like their fellow-journalists on competing newspapers, they work as a team, under the immediate and critical eye of their superiors and equals and under the inexorable eye of the clock. Under these glaring conditions a man's faults, weaknesses and mistakes will show up like a misprint in a headline. It takes a good man to hold down a key job in the *Daily Mirror*. The men who are continuously concerned in the daily production of the paper are very much less concerned with its direction and aim. Not that they generally disapprove of its politics, for instance, or disregard its impact on 14·75 million readers. But they are working newspapermen, and their time and energies are completely taken up by the exacting technique of their exacting jobs. They don't worry so much about the possible effects of the *Mirror* as about the practical problems of the next edition.

The Mirror and Its Readers

All papers make a practice of printing letters from their readers, favourable and unfavourable. A letter attacking the paper not only gives a public impression that the editors are tolerant and fair-minded men who believe in free speech and act on their belief; it also makes the editors themselves feel that their shoulders are broad and can stand a certain amount of belabouring. Often a critical letter, if its tone is friendly, can even serve as a kind of back-handed advertisement of the paper.

In the days of the "tabloid revolution" the *Mirror* ran this letter from a reader: "You write too much about society nobodies. You also write too much about ordinary nobodies. You flash people up in enormous type just because they are young and in love or old and out of love, because they live extravagantly or die horribly. What will you do when something important happens? Burst?" The *Mirror* printed this letter, apparently, in much the same spirit in which Mr. Toad sang songs in praise of himself—because he felt such affection for his own shortcomings that he easily convinced himself they were not shortcomings at all but hearty and attractive qualities. The *Mirror* likes itself and makes no bones about it; and its readers share the liking and applaud the feeling.

The *Mirror* has more young readers (from 16 to 35) than any other paper. This fact is not necessarily a reflection on British youth: Cecil King claims that it is a result of deliberate foresight. In the fierce struggle for readers it is not enough to win the support of millions; as they grow older or die or drift away their ranks must be continually replenished, and the sensible long view is not to count on luring deserters from other papers but to recruit new readers who never bought a paper before. The grammar schools still turn them out, and in greater numbers than in Northcliffe's day. Not content with the lion's share of 16- to-35-year-olds, the *Mirror* wants to condition even younger readers to the *Mirror* habit. This was the rationale behind much of the Mirror's "prestige advertising" (the children's art shows, children's orchestra, etc.) and behind the short-lived *Junior Mirror*. This Sunday paper for the kiddies and the young-in-heart was started in 1954 and dropped the next year, but it had perhaps served its purpose by frightening the *Express* into following suit with a *Junior Express*. And the *Mirror* still had a bigger share of youthful readers than any of its competitors.

The Royal Commission on the Press pointed out that there is a "subtle relationship" between a newspaper and its readers. The *Mirror* tries and thinks it succeeds in making its relationship with its readers as little subtle, as frank and as close as possible. No newspaper has courted its readers more assiduously; few have spent as much time and thought in trying to find out their likes and dislikes, hopes and fears. The *Mirror* encourages its readers to speak up, on any excuse or none. Most of the letters they write are answered, and never with a formal "Dear Sir" or "Dear Madam" but always with the writer's own name. Replies to women readers are written in longhand, because the *Mirror* is convinced that women don't like typewritten letters. Of the hundreds of letters that come in every day from readers, the *Mirror* has room to print only a score, with or without comment. A strong indication that the *Mirror's* relations with its readers are indeed close is the fact (or the belief, strongly held by the *Mirror's* editors) that the most popular feature in the paper is "Live Letters", the department in which the anonymous Old Codgers answer or comment on a dozen or so letters a day.

When Mass Observation was trying to find out what paper various people read, and why, a 30-year-old waitress gave this answer: "I like any bloody paper that has the horseracing results in." Well, she could find them in the *Mirror*, but the *Mirror* wouldn't like her cynically undiscriminating attitude. Being a daily entertainment with a serious purpose behind it, the more the *Mirror* can identify itself with the interests of working-class readers, the more readers it will have and the more powerful it will become. Horseracing results alone are too tenuous a thread to tie a reader to the *Mirror*; the great mass of its following have more in common with the paper than that.

Besides looking at their favourite features, more than half the *Mirror's* readers even like to read the news. They're not expected to read the whole paper—no newspaper reader ever does that—but in the six minutes the *Mirror* is in their hands most of them are daily reassured in the feeling that the *Mirror* is a bright, warm-hearted, helpful friend.

Who Owns the Daily Mirror?

For purposes best known to himself, Beaverbrook has sometimes tried to create a mystery about the ownership of the *Mirror*. His *Evening Standard* repeatedly hinted that financial control of the *Mirror* was in the hands of Mr. Israel Sieff, a director of Marks & Spencer. Other rumours have arisen from time to time: that the *Mirror* was being bought by a syndicate, one of whose members was J. Arthur Rank, the cinema magnate; that William Randolph Hearst, the late American Press tycoon, was a large shareholder. Mentioning no names but simply raising the sinister question, the Communist *Daily Worker* has spread what suspicion it could: "Who is behind the *Daily Mirror*, the paper that shouts 'Forward with the People' and stabs every actual people's movement in the back?"

None of these hints or rumours was true. In fact, the *Mirror's* shares are so widely held that no single individual owns a controlling interest. The largest block of *Mirror* shares, about 20%, is owned by the *Sunday Pictorial*—whose shares, in turn, are about 24% owned by the *Mirror*. The Royal Commission on the Press, which thoroughly investigated the ownership of the *Mirror*, reported that "the practical effect of this is that the directors of the two companies[1] can exercise absolute control". Since three of the five *Mirror* directors are also on the six-man board of the *Pictorial*, this constitutes an interlocking directorate—or, as *Investors' Chronicle* has put it, "both the head and tail of the fortunate dog can wag each other at will".[2]

The Chairman of both companies is Cecil Harmsworth King. He does not own a controlling financial interest in the Mirror, though he is reputed to be the second-largest shareholder and also to hold the proxy of the largest single shareholder, Sir John Reeves Ellerman. As long as the two companies (in effect, one company) continue to make money and as long as his fellow-directors are satisfied with the job he does as Chairman, Cecil King is the boss and will continue to be. And, in the words of his Editorial Director, Hugh Cudlipp, "the financial record of the company has always been impressive, and often a source of delight to its stockholders."

Net profit of the two companies for the year ending in February, 1957, was £1,284,643.

In the year ending in February 1956 the Mirror made most of its profits (96·3%) from investments; only 3·7% came from net trading profit (newspaper publication). This was an unusual year, as the *Mirror* had been hard hit by the printing strike and a railway strike; in the year ending in February, 1957, the *Mirror* made £924,694 from net trading profit and £290,828 from investments.

The Mirror and the Rest of the Press

The *Daily Mirror* is regarded by the rest of the Press with contempt, envy, hatred, amusement, alarm and admiration—

[1] The Daily Mirror Newspapers Ltd., The Sunday Pictorial Newspapers Ltd.

[2] Referring to the Press in general but perhaps with the *Daily Mirror* particularly in mind, a broadsheet on The State of the Press issued (September 1935) by Political and Economic Planning said: "The financial structure of the Press is in fact more complicated than that of the great majority of British industries, and this complexity lays it open to the suspicion of being unsound. In some cases interlocking shareholdings make it impossible for anyone except those who exercise it even to discover where the actual control rests."

in short, with very mixed feelings. As might be expected, the loftiest scorn is expressed by the more conservative, small-circulation papers whose politics are right-wing, the bitterest hatred by mass-circulation papers which compete with the *Mirror*, and by those elements in the left-wing Press which are committed to a party line. The *Manchester Guardian*, which could hardly be more respectable, has a soft spot in its heart for the *Mirror*; and the *New Statesman*, which could hardly be more top-lofty and doctrinaire, almost always stands up for the *Mirror* when somebody else is attacking it. The *Mirror's* most relentless enemies are the left-wing weekly *Tribune* and the right-wing daily *Sketch*, with the Communist *Daily Worker* close behind.

Here are some sample nosegays from *Tribune*: "Mr. Hugh Cudlipp, hitherto acclaimed on all sides as the Cheesecake King of Fleet Street, is also the master of a gangster journalism which Mr. Christiansen [Editor of the *Daily Express*] will never be able to equal, no matter how hard he tries. . . . Mr. Hugh Cudlipp, Managing Director of the *Daily Mirror*, has been attempting the defence of those papers which make handsome profits by debauching our adolescents: a gallant spectacle, like Touchstone's knight defending the honour which he had not. Mr. Cudlipp's main arguments seem to be two. The first is that you must give the public what it wants. This is the classic defence of prostitution, and presumably not even Mr. Cudlipp wishes to take it to its logical conclusion, which is the decline and fall of the Roman Empire. The second line of defence is that these papers reflect life as it is. If Mr. Cudlipp believes this, which I doubt, I can only suggest that he has been reading the *Daily Mirror* for so long that he has reduced himself to the state in which he wishes to see everyone else." Even *Tribune*, however, sometimes gives the devil his due: "When it comes to explaining political problems in plain man's language, all the party propagandists can take a lesson from the *Daily Mirror*."

When the august *Sunday Times* (which calls itself independent but is in fact Conservative) deigns to notice the *Mirror*, it is usually in a fleeting and anonymous reference—"the wildness of a yellow tabloid". But the *Daily Sketch*, a less successful sensational tabloid than the *Mirror*, attacks its enemy directly. Sometimes, in its eagerness to score, the *Sketch* gives away one of the dirtier tricks of the trade, a trick not always confined to tabloids:

> The *Daily Mirror* is at it again.
>
> It tries to justify its campaign against Anthony Eden. It denounces its critics as "cloth-eared". Well, that kind of abuse won't hurt anybody.
>
> But the latest attack is another example of the *Mirror's* methods. Under the guise of defending itself it repeats the allegations it made last week.
>
> Once more it prints details of Anthony Eden's private life. Once more it prints the completely phoney story that this is a subject of public controversy.
>
> Once more it adds unctuously that, of course, the *Mirror* does not believe such an issue should affect Anthony Eden's fitness to succeed Churchill.

The *Mirror's* less-than-reverential attitude toward the Royal Family, and particularly its nudging curiosity about Princess Margaret, has roused the ire of various journals, particularly among the Church Press. The *Methodist Recorder* deplored "the tactics of the *Daily Mirror* in calling for a poll of its readers on the personal affairs of Princess Margaret.... The only obvious conclusion is that this newspaper, which by the number of its comic strips must have many half-literate readers, will go a long way in the search for sensation." The same poll was condemned by the *Church of England Newspaper* as "the cheapest kind of tenth-rate gutter journalism . . . invites the contempt of decent men. A newspaper which has shown itself capable of greatness ought to consider it unworthy of its dignity."

But the *Church of England Newspaper* cannot long disguise its wistful feeling that the *Mirror* is not a black sheep but an erring one, perhaps even a sheep-dog in disguise: "It must be admitted, and that without explanation or diffidence, that the *Daily Mirror* has a certain fascination for the *Church of England Newspaper*. . . . Reading the *Daily Mirror* is like eavesdropping on a few men and some girls chatting in a public-house. It has the same good points and the same faults. It has the same kindliness, the same sentimentality, the same crudity, the same vulgarity, the same prying curiosity, the same prejudices, and the same interests. . . . Whatever else may be said of the *Daily Mirror* there is no denying it has guts. . . . Not everything the *Daily Mirror* does is wrong. In fact on occasion it speaks out in a remarkably fine and forthright way."

Only very rarely can its critics manage to laugh at the *Mirror*, but it has happened. The *Eastern Daily Press* once referred to it as "the *Daily Mirror*, which nails its colours firmly to the weathercock". A much commoner tone is one not of light mockery but heavy jeering, as in this passage in the *Spectator*: "I am sorry to see the *Daily Mirror* losing its political touch. It has always been pleasant to know that, whether in jail[1] or out of it, its anonymous political clowns would find the only way of making the Janes of the country vote Labour."

Oddly enough, the severest strictures on the British popular Press in general and the *Mirror* in particular (though usually by inference) come from the U.S. Press. Said the Washington *Post*: "The *Times* of London is a credit to any country. The vigorous *Manchester Guardian* . . . deservedly enjoys a reputation as one of the world's best newspapers. The *Daily Telegraph*, the *Observer*, the *Sunday Times*—these are serious publications which do a competent job of informing their readers about world affairs. But the common denominator of London journalism, which is national journalism, is lower than even the most sensational papers in this country". Roscoe Drummond, writing in the New York *Herald Tribune*, said: "Journalistically, I find

[1] A reference to the three-months prison sentence of a former Editor of the *Mirror*, Sylvester Bolam, for contempt of court.

Britain unexcelled at two points. Its best newspapers are among the very best in the world. Its worst newspapers are the worst newspapers anywhere. . . . On the debit side of British journalism is the awful paucity of solid news in most popular and tabloid picture newspapers. We Americans often think the British Press neglects America; I think that most British mass-circulation newspapers neglect what is important about Britain. The mass-circulation British Press is a sensational, restless hodge-podge of trash and trivia decorated with rather undraped bathing beauties and the more glamorous movie stars. It has 50,000,000 Britons to work on and it works on them to no good purpose."

There have also been soberer and more balanced criticisms of the *Mirror*. John Beavan, formerly London Editor of the *Manchester Guardian* and now Assistant Director of the Nuffield Foundation, found much good in the *Mirror* and some bad: "Few newspapers except the *Daily Mirror* have found that the world has changed. . . . The *Mirror* says a lot in a very few words. And it is very easy to grasp the point the *Daily Mirror* is making. . . . I think it succeeded because it is the first newspaper which has really got into the kitchens of working-class houses. . . . The *Daily Mirror* accepts people as they are, crude, sentimental, self-sacrificing, selfish—all the contradictions of human nature. . . . There is much in that newspaper I loathe, and I deplore the effect its success has had on other newspapers. Nevertheless, I feel it has discovered something of great value—of greater value than the paper itself seems to realise. . . . The *Mirror* is a very important newspaper in English life and it cannot be neglected."

And the *Socialist Leader* had this to say: "An excellent guide to the violent loves and three-dimensional excitement of this modern age, the *Daily Mirror*, Britain's top-selling daily, is an enthusiast for lush and unabashedly seductive girls with well-contoured bodies and dental work made into touching items, dame-chasers with crew-cuts, and the incredible ugliness of synthetic living. It reports succinctly on sensuous beauties—

on their past glories and present states of exhilaration or decay, and often portrays them as angels of simplicity. It delves deep into the undergrowth of the jungle of the big city; it thrives on illiteracy and superstition and revels in savagery. No sorrow is too harrowing, no misery too painful for it to exploit. It is a plant nurtured in Fleet Street that blossoms in the arid wastes of back-street slums and the poisoned atmosphere of Mayfair gin-parlours. To people willing to wade through a morass of garbage to see the grimness and dross of this age, the *Mirror* offers ample directions. All this is generally conceded, except, perhaps, by the *Mirror* itself."

The *Mirror* takes a positive delight in repeating almost anything and everything critical that is said about it, and the more outrageous the better. Hard words, the *Mirror* feels, will never hurt it; on the contrary, they give it a lot of free advertising and further its reputation as a fearless, brash, two-fisted tabloid.

Indeed, the *Mirror* loves to feature these attacks. Not long ago it printed one of them every day for a week or so, in big black type at the top of page 2—e.g., "The MIRROR—by TRIBUNE (these words appeared in a political weekly, *Tribune*): 'The *Mirror* chooses to run everybody else's business. It tells the Labour Party what leaders to choose. It instructs Princess Margaret when to get married.' "

Or it quotes Aneurin Bevan, that the *Mirror* is "the least reputable among newspapers", and then points out with a grin that Mr. Bevan had recently written a series of articles for the *Mirror* and been well paid for them. At the height of the row (mainly stirred up by the *Mirror*) over the Press treatment of Princess Margaret and Captain Townsend, the *Mirror* reprinted the *News Chronicle's* disgusted remarks: "The *Daily Mirror* . . . succeeded in plumbing hitherto unreached depths of self-importance, impertinence and plain bad manners . . . at the expense of someone who, by the nature of her position, cannot defend herself or answer back"—and followed them by quoting the *New Statesman*: "The *Mirror* says openly only what readers of the *News Chronicle* and the *Manchester Guardian* whisper behind their hands."

Whether or not the *Mirror* is right in feeling that this kind of advertising does it no harm and may even do some good by getting the paper talked about, it can afford to indulge itself in such thick-skinned pleasures. Its real answer to all the brick-bats is: look at the circulation figures. When the 1956 I.P.A. survey showed the *Mirror* leading all British daily newspapers by more than a million (14·75 million to the *Express's* 12·58), the *Mirror* exulted: "Why is the *Mirror* still The Champ? We believe it is because the bond between readers and this newspaper is unique. The *Mirror* speaks in the language of the people. It isn't pompous or highfalutin. We deal with life as it is—and not as the intellectuals or moralists would like it to be."

PART III

THE MANCHESTER GUARDIAN:
SCOTT TO WADSWORTH

THE *Manchester Guardian* was born on May 5, 1821, the same day Napoleon died on St. Helena. This dates the *Guardian* in more ways than one, for in its first number the paper reported the ex-Emperor in good health. (It was not until July that news of his death reached the British Press.) The founder of the *Guardian*, John Edward Taylor, the son of a Quaker schoolmaster, was a solid Manchester citizen and a Whig: he wished the paper to be a commercial success—and until that was assured he could not get married, which he very much wanted to do—but he intended it also to be an instrument of Parliamentary and social reform.

Britain's only daily papers in those days were published in London, and the *Guardian* began as a weekly of four pages. There were already six weeklies in Manchester, and one of them had been going for 70 years. In spite of this competition, and although it was not very different from its competitors, the *Guardian* was a success from the start. It gave more emphasis than was usual to the leading article and was the first to have its own reporter, Jeremiah Garnett, who was also its printer and business manager. In twelve years the *Guardian* had the largest circulation in Manchester—something over 3,000.

Newspapers in those days were expensive. The main cause was the Government "taxes on knowledge": a stamp for every copy sold, taxes on advertisements and paper. The *Guardian's* original price was 7*d.* a copy, of which 4*d.* went to the Government. The tax was designed to restrict newspapers: the Government distrusted the lower orders and feared that cheap papers would flatter their prejudices and "espouse their peculiar views, how inconsistent soever these may be with the interests of society in general". Society in general, however, wanted cheaper papers, and decided to risk their peculiar views: gradually the taxes were lowered and finally, in 1855, abolished. The immediate result was a sudden flowering of morning papers in the provinces. The *Guardian*, like many others, became a daily and dropped its price to 2*d*., then to a penny.

Meantime the *Guardian's* first editor had been succeeded by his son, who died at 24, and then by Jeremiah Garnett, the reporter-printer. In 1861 John Edward Taylor the second, another son of the founder, became editor. Though the paper was now a daily with a circulation of more than 20,000, the mid-Victorian atmosphere of its offices was still unhurried. "It was the product of long, leisurely afternoons. Its leader-writers withheld their hands from the news of the current night and went home, like barristers, on reasonable evening trains." It was becoming known as a sound and thoughtful provincial newspaper. Its reputation grew to national stature in the Franco-Prussian War of 1870, when the *Guardian* had its own war correspondents, three with the French and one with the Germans.[1] The following year the *Guardian* was joined by a young Oxford graduate who was to make it internationally famous.

Charles Prestwich Scott, a nephew by marriage of the *Guardian's* first editor and cousin of the contemporary editor-proprietor, was an extraordinarily handsome and uncompromisingly noble young man. Brought up in a well-to-do family of high-minded Dissenters, he had been educated at private schools and at Oxford—Corpus Christi was tolerant enough to stretch a point and admit a non-Anglican. He had taken a First in Greats in 1869, and had then served a brief apprenticeship in journalism on *The Scotsman*. A year after he came to the *Guardian* his cousin appointed him Editor. He was 25.

At Oxford, Scott had made up his mind that he would

[1] One of them had sent despatches out of beleaguered Metz by small balloons; each was labelled with a request to the finder to forward it to the *Manchester Guardian*, which would pay the forwarder £10.

dedicate his life to some sort of public service, and it was in this spirit that he became the *Guardian's* editor. Since he entered journalism at the top, without having gone through the run-of-the-mill reporting assignments that season and shape most newspapermen, the bond of shared experience was lacking between him and the men he worked with. Add to that lack his position, his youth, and the icy fire of his nature, and it becomes evident why the relations between Scott and his staff were not only formal but fearsome. As the years went by, there was no lessening of formality and the fearsomeness increased.

At first, however, as a very youthful and completely untried editor at the head of an experienced staff, he seems to have guided the paper with a fairly loose rein. In the early years of his editorship he himself wrote very little. But he was determined to develop and improve the *Guardian's* quality, and he would not tolerate bad writing. As he wrote many years later: "People talk of 'journalese', as though a journalist were of necessity a pretentious and sloppy writer; he may be, on the contrary, and very often is, one of the best in the world. At least, he should not be content to be much less."

The calibre of the journalists Scott gathered round him may be seen from the names of some of the men who became members of the *Guardian* staff in his day or who wrote for the paper, often anonymously: Andrew Lang, George Saintsbury, John Masefield, William Archer, Laurence Housman, Sturge Moore, H. W. Massingham, H. W. Nevinson, John Drinkwater, Clutton Brock, H. N. Brailsford, Lowes Dickinson, James Agate, Maurice Hewlett, J. M. Keynes, L. S. Amery, Arthur Ransome, Arnold Toynbee, J. M. Synge, W. T. Stead.

The man who set the tone for *Guardian* writers in Scott's early years was William Thomas Arnold, grandson of Arnold of Rugby. Scott recruited him from Oxford to be chief leader-writer, and he became one of the men, like C. E. Montague after him, who made the *Guardian* famous.

[W. T. Arnold] may be taken as the true founder of the

genre school of *Guardian* writers. . . . The drama of the town, and even in course of time its music-halls of Empire and Hippodrome, its picture galleries and loan exhibitions, its concerts, its Whit-week, its Zoological Gardens at Belle Vue, and all its encircling scenery of Cheshire and Derbyshire became, under the stimulus of his first example, the subject matter of a critical attitude, a descriptiveness and a habit of hard writing resolving themselves into a familiar style highly literary but never bookish, and the spiritual secret of which is a slight disdain of London, an austere contentment with the object before the eye, and a grim determination to write before the end of life more or less like Montague.

Scott himself never aspired to write like that, although eventually he made his "unburnished and uncajoling style" (in C. E. Montague's phrase) "a powerful instrument of persuasion". But he wanted that kind of writing in the paper, and he picked his critical staff with great care, solely for their literary ability and knowledge of their field. Their political or religious beliefs might be completely alien to Scott's, and often were. Some of his most prized contributors were extreme Conservatives; one was a Roman Catholic prelate, another an anarchist. The leader page, the voice of the *Guardian*, was another matter. There the mind and the moral position were necessarily consonant with Scott's. As Editor, he was the keeper of the *Guardian's* conscience, as he later became its embodiment and chief spokesman.

Scott never forgot nor let his staff forget that the *Guardian* was not to be like other papers. It had assumed a responsibility and elected a role that put it, if not quite in a class by itself, at any rate in a small group whose members competed for excellence rather than for popularity. As he wrote on the paper's hundredth anniversary: "A newspaper has two sides to it. It is a business, like any other, and has to pay in the material sense in order to live. But it is much more than a business; it is an institution; it reflects and it influences the life of a whole community; it may affect even wider destinies. It is, in its way, an instrument of government. It plays on the minds and consciences of men. It may educate, stimulate, assist, or it may do the opposite. It has, therefore, a moral as well as a material existence, and its character and influence are in the main determined by the balance of these two forces. It may make profit or power its first object, or it may conceive itself as fulfilling a higher and more exacting function. . . ."

Scott admired Gladstone as the most moral politician of the day, and when in 1886 the Grand Old Man was converted to Home Rule for Ireland and the Liberal Party was split, Scott and the *Guardian* followed Gladstone. Gladstonian Liberalism ("the precise and exact opposite of Prussianism") was an uncompromising and northerly creed: "it inured those who followed it to the unpleasant process of thinking and acting against the grain of a facile patriotism, and living in allegiance to that other country which is also theirs and is bounded on the north, the south, the east and the west, not by political frontiers, but by the moral idea". This dual citizenship led Scott into some very unpopular positions and let the *Guardian* in for some rough passages. Before and during the Boer War, the *Guardian* "was set inflexibly against the national will. . . . The paper needed all its roots in the family life of Manchester, in its commerce, its markets, its churches, its music and art and sport to survive the weather which beat upon it during the South African War." At one point feeling ran so high against Scott and his paper that the Manchester authorities insisted on putting a police cordon around the *Guardian* offices—"to protect it and him from his readers". This amazed and amused Scott, who was always perfectly oblivious to personal danger. He was not so much courageous as fearless.

It was a "serious thing to take an organism at once large and delicate, a complicated affair of buildings and machinery, of gathered capital and goodwill like the *Manchester Guardian* and place it right across the path of public fury. But this is what Scott proceeded fearlessly to do. . . . The *Manchester Guardian* and a solid block of its constituency began at this period their long course of training in the art of agreeing to differ, or perhaps we might say in the art of not differing except in opinion. Scott, as a journalist, evolved a new kind of 'Constant Reader' whose constancy connoted an imperfect degree of discipleship."

He was just as disregarding of personal friendship when principle was at stake. He supported, liked and in some ways admired Lloyd George,[1] but in 1921, when Lloyd George was Prime Minister and the "trouble" in Ireland was at its height, "day after day Scott returned to the subject, and nobody who follows the history of that time will doubt that the blows Mr. Lloyd George received from his friend were the hardest that he had to bear. Scott put into these articles all the power that his self-control gave to his indignation, and if the Government was gradually borne down by the pressure of moral opinion, Scott's pen was one of the chief forces in putting an end to the terror of the Black and Tans."

Formal and cool as he was in personal relations, the problems of far-off or unseen people brought out in him an amazingly penetrating sympathy. His political conscience, especially on foreign issues, became almost as dependable as a compass needle. Though he was incapable of autobiography he once modestly hinted at his method: "The first condition of a real understanding is perhaps a sympathetic approach. . . . Not that the task is easy. What, in fact, can be more difficult than really to enter into the mind of a man of another nation, still more to grasp the conditions which go to make him what he is—his education, the atmosphere of his home, the traditions of his people. Yet it is all these things which, when the test comes, go to determine his outlook and his action. It is for the Press, so far as it may, to act as interpreter, and one of its first duties is to qualify for the task. . . ."

[1] His admiration for Lloyd George was mixed, however. Scott backed him as much and as often as his conscience would allow, partly because he considered Lloyd George the hope of the Liberal Party. Nevertheless, Scott recognised his trickiness and in private once referred to him as a liar—but for all that, said Scott, quite sincere: he simply made different statements at different times, persuading himself each time that this was what he believed.

How well Scott qualified himself may be seen by a comparison of the *Guardian's* record with the *Times'*, for example: on every important issue of this century in which the *Times* supported the Government and the *Guardian* opposed it (e.g., the Irish question, the Boer War, women's suffrage, the Versailles Treaty), the nation as a whole eventually came around to the *Guardian's* view. This could hardly be attributed to the *Guardian's* influence; it points rather to the probability that on these questions the *Guardian* really represented, as the *Times* did not, the conscience of the nation.

Since he felt so conscientious about politics, it was natural that Scott should have wanted to play a more direct political part than he could as an editor. In 1895 he stood for Parliament as Liberal Member for the Leigh Division of Lancashire, and won a seat which he kept for ten years. But he was too uncompromising for party politics, and in Parliament, where he belonged to the "minority of a minority", he was too close to his audience to be effective. Moreover, he was not a good speaker, especially in front of a hostile crowd. "His habit of waiting in a state of suspended animation until he was visited by the word he wanted produced tingling silences even before sympathetic audiences."

While he was in Parliament Scott continued to act as Editor and spent as much time in Manchester as he could. But this was a far from perfect arrangement, and ten years of it were more than enough. In 1905 his political and his private life both came to an end: with the death of J. E. Taylor, the *Guardian's* proprietor, Scott became the owner as well as Editor of the paper; and when his wife died in the same year, the *Guardian* became his life. He was now 60; but the best of his career was still before him. Until he was 84, Scott was the absolute governor of the *Guardian*, and wrote most of the important leaders. His days and a large part of each night were completely filled with work.

He lived in a simple but fairly large and comfortable house, The Firs, on what were then the outskirts of Manchester. There each morning he got a copy of the *Guardian*, in which every anonymous article and news item was marked with the name of its writer or its source. After his cold bath and a breakfast of raw fruit he set to work on his massive correspondence and was at it all day, with a break for lunch and an hour's bicycling in the afternoon. After tea, which he liked to brew himself, he wrote more letters; and shortly before seven set off on his bicycle for the six-mile ride to the office and the evening's work. This usually included the writing of a long leader, against "a dropping fire of interruptions from his staff."

When he had finished he bicycled home to an 11 o'clock supper—generally raw fruit again. He was a famous figure in the Manchester streets: a spare, square, erect old man with silky white hair and beard, dressed in a cap, norfolk jacket, plus fours and high buttoned boots. In winter he added a muffler, but no overcoat. Between his nightly rides to and from the office and his afternoon excursions, "very little in the life of Manchester escaped Scott's attention . . . if the Corporation, pushing out a new tram-line, threatened in its haste to uproot a row of elms, as likely as not it was he, out in the afternoon on his bicycle, who detected the villainy, and his pen which returned to the subject night after night, engendering considerable heat".

On nights when he expected to be working later than usual he would bring his supper, of bread, cheese and fruit, to the office, and set a pot of butter on the ledge outside his window. Not till he was 78, was blind in one eye and had had several bad falls and near-fatal collisions did his family prevail on him to give up his nightly bicycle trips. Neville Cardus tells a story (which Scott is supposed to have retailed himself) of a policeman who picked him up one night after he had skidded in the slush, and remonstrated with him for being out so late in such bad weather. When Scott explained that he had been working at the *Guardian*, the policeman exploded, "Well, all I can say is this, sir: the *Manchester Guardian* ought to be bloody well ashamed of itself keeping an old man like you out this time of the night." He looked frail, but wasn't. "Nobody dared complain of weariness to Scott", says Cardus. "Illness he could not understand, though he tried sympathetically to get one's point of view." Hamilton Owens, former editor of the Baltimore *Sun*, remembers "his proud, stern face and his burning eyes, like those of an avenging angel. . . ." Once, when he was 80, he took the night train to London, after his evening's work at the office, had breakfast with Lloyd George, a lengthy interview with Venizelos, and lunch with Lord Cecil; he returned to Manchester by the afternoon train, went back to the office and wrote the main leader that evening.[1]

Scott's confident serenity was irritating to some, awe-inspiring to others. He was always sure that England would come around to doing her duty as he saw it. His nature was so sanguine that he could always accept a reverse as temporary. He was so forward-looking, indeed, that it was next to impossible to make him talk about the irretrievable past. James Bone, who occasionally tried it, said admiringly, "It was wonderful the way he could change the subject, in two sentences, and be telling you enthusiastically about a new method of surfacing roads in Manchester, and how it was bound to make revolutionary changes. He was always getting out from the past and away to the future!"

The sensational success of popular journalism left him unmoved. "The first stage in the organisation of universal education in England had created a very large new reading public, half-educated, credulous, excitable, and ready to lend itself to neurotic joint movements, under the influence of journalistic suggestion, like those dangerous bodily swayings which can so easily be started in standing crowds." Many of his fellow-editors feared that the only way newspapers could survive was to lower their standards and cater to this new audience. But "to exploit popular ignorance, to play up to the vices or weaknesses

[1] On another occasion, when Scott was going to London to dine with Lloyd George and discuss the Irish crisis, then at its height, he wrote a leader on the subject *before* leaving Manchester—and afterwards never changed a word. This scrupulousness above and beyond the call of journalistic duty was characteristic of Scott.

of half-formed characters and half-filled minds would have seemed to him a policy no more worth considering than a policy of living on the profits of disorderly houses".

In 1921, the centenary of the *Guardian's* founding and the 50th year of Scott's editorship, the whole nation, regardless of creed and party, congratulated him and, by implication, themselves. The King sent a telegram acknowledging his "courage and high-mindedness". Lord Curzon, the great Tory, magnanimously recognised the force and fairness with which Scott had expressed views opposed to Curzon's—i.e., wrong. Lord Robert Cecil supplied the phrase of the moment: Scott had made righteousness readable. The lesser breeds sent their tributes too.

Twelve years later, when he died at 87, the chorus of praise swelled even louder. Lloyd George called him "the noblest figure in modern journalism." The Russian Ambassador telegraphed: "The name of the *Manchester Guardian* stands as one of the very few organs which told to the world the truth about the Russian Revolution and the work of reconstruction in the Soviet Union." President Cosgrave of Ireland declared that "his services to Ireland will long be remembered by my countrymen." J. L. Garvin wrote: "A great man and greatest of all editors, he ennobled his age." The Conservative *Morning Post* granted that "he personified in himself and through the newspaper which he controlled and gave voice to, the Radical conscience of the English nation. . . . The standard which he set in British journalism was as absolute as the British pound, and its maintenance was a national service which must eclipse all political perversities." The *Observer* called him "the greatest and in every way the best of all recorded editors. . . . Scott always lifted the argument." The New York *Times* announced that "for many years the *Manchester Guardian* has been regarded both at home and abroad as the most influential newspaper in England." And among the many telegrams was one from the King, from Prime Minister Ramsay MacDonald, and from Gandhi.

Besides these formal tributes there is more intimate evidence about him. It is not damaging evidence, nor even very diminishing, but it does change his shape a little. Scott's unfailing courtesy was of a formidably old-fashioned kind, punctilious, demanding, cold as steel. Although he neither smoked nor drank, he always had wine on the table for his guests and would take one sip himself; after lunch he would pass around cigarettes, light one himself and then let it go out. As soon as the guests had left he would fling the remains of his cigarette into the fireplace, exclaiming, "A *filthy* habit!" There is a photograph of the old man at a family birthday party: he is actually wearing a paper hat, and at the slight angle which paper hats are prone to assume; but there is nothing either silly or gay in his appearance. He looks as if he were challenging anyone to laugh, and quite sure that no one will accept the challenge. He was known to laugh himself, but his laughter was apt to be of the sort which euphemism calls "kindly".

W. P. Crozier, who later became Editor of the *Guardian*, said that Scott ruled his staff with absolute authority and "an almost military discipline but he did not like it said so". Scott was, in effect, a tyrant, and, as such, he had to be humoured. Crozier tells of one such time-wasting fuss at the *Guardian* office: "Over a photograph of the infant Princess Elizabeth being driven in a car with her nurse, he pondered for some time. The Princess was certainly admissible, but he knew nothing about the nurse, and it seemed too much prominence for a woman who had made no mark on his consciousness. A few hastily remembered facts about the nurse's long service with the Bowes-Lyon family were laid before him, together with the impossibility of blotting her out of the picture and leaving her charge unblemished, and he finally agreed that a modestly-sized reproduction should be given."

As Scott grew older some of his regular habits developed into crotchets—but crotchets with the force of immutable law. After his wife's death his youngest son Edward, at that time his only married son, and his family lived with him for several years. There was only one bathroom in the house. Scott's invariable custom was to start the day with an icy-cold bath, and to ensure its iciness the bath was always drawn the night before and left standing, with the window open—even in winter. His daughter-in-law liked her bath (hot) in the evening, so she used to empty out the cold water she found there and draw another cold bath before she left. Nothing was ever said about this rearrangement, but she was quite certain that he always knew what had happened because he found his bath not cold enough. Neither side gave an inch. When another bathroom was put in, on the excuse of an imminent visit from an American journalist, the impasse was finally solved.

As a young man, Professor David Mitrany worked closely with Scott for several years on the editorial staff, specialising in foreign affairs, and grew to love and revere him. But he too once had to humour the old man into doing the sensible thing. Edward Scott was about to become Editor—at least nominally—in his father's place, and Mitrany was urging on Edward and his wife the value, indeed the necessity, before he settled down to the grindstone, of taking a three-month trip to see for himself the new, post-war Europe of Masaryk, Mussolini, Kemal, etc. Edward agreed that such a trip would be very much worth while, but said sadly that the old man would never let him go for that long. Mitrany said, "Will you let me try?" On his next meeting with C. P. Scott he brought up the subject casually, referring to it as an obviously good idea—"but of course", he added, "his wife will never let him go." Scott, banging his hand on the table: "He must go! I will persuade her." Later Scott reported to Mitrany that he had been able to talk his daughter-in-law round.

The *Guardian* staff, almost without exception, admired Scott to the point of awe. Neville Cardus wrote in his *Autobiography*: "I cannot believe that any *Guardian* man ever knocked at a door behind which Scott waited for him and did not feel a need to pull himself together." But few seem to have loved him. Some, especially those who left the paper, were outspoken in their resentment of Scott's coldness and aloofness. One of these,

Howard Spring, wrote that in his eleven years on the *Guardian* he had never had a word of praise or dispraise from the Editor. "Scott lacked more completely than any man I have ever known the human touch that turns a partisan into a devotee. I cannot think of any man that I would die for; but, in any list of possibles, C. P. Scott's name would be near the bottom. . . . He lacked the common touch—which makes a good or bad epitaph as you read it."

Apparently without giving them much choice in the matter, Scott dedicated the lives of both his sons to the service of the *Guardian*. His daughter married C. E. Montague, who was Scott's right-hand man and who must have hoped for a time to be his successor. Montague was a man of tremendous reserve, as Scott was a man of impregnable formality, and Montague never so much as hinted at the disappointment he must have felt. In spite of their close family ties and their long companionship on the *Guardian*, there is no record of a scene between these two that was either angry or affectionate.

Scott, said W. P. Crozier, "liked people to feel deeply, think clearly, and hold themselves in". It was a rule he applied to himself first and foremost. A lifetime of controlled feeling and whetted thinking built up in him a power which sometimes exerted the force of poetry. He once said that "the most wonderful thing in the world is the jet of life in a little child".

Though C. P. Scott, in turn the boy wonder, father superior and oldest inhabitant of the *Guardian*, accumulated a towering reputation, there was a period when C. E. Montague's name was perhaps equally well known. Scott's writing went anonymously and entirely into his paper, while Montague published signed articles and wrote half a dozen widely read books—the best-known, *Disenchantment*, one of the few first-rate personal accounts of the 1914-18 war.

Charles Edward Montague was the third son of an Irish ex-priest; after Oxford, where he was a Scholar of Balliol,[1] he

[1] A circumstance that may have given currency to the saying that only a Scholar of Balliol could hope to get a job on the *Guardian*.

joined the *Guardian* staff in 1890. Eight years later he married Scott's only daughter Madeline, by whom he had seven children—five sons and two daughters. A solemn-looking man of medium height with a long Irish upper lip and large patient ears, Montague wanted above all things to be an excellent writer. Whether he succeeded or ever could have succeeded in achieving the style of which his whole life was a dogged pursuit is an open question. He did perfect a manner of writing—or a mannered way of writing—which was admired in its day but has now gone completely out of fashion. Even in the large liberty of the *Guardian*, where every writer's idiosyncrasies were given at least elbow-room, Montague may have felt cramped. Perhaps an example of his unfettered style, when he was writing exactly as he pleased, may show why: "There are things not to be put on the stage; a lady killing her infants, a king putting out his own eyes—better take them as seen; one yell, if you will, from a child 'off', to keep your fancy at work, one waft of sound from where Oedipus damns and blasts in the wings as he rams in the pin; but no more, blood is fine, but it pays to go straight to the more delectable mess that is made of the souls of the principals. No disrespect to suppers of horrors; only of two, hold out for the squarer."

That kind of thing would never do in a leader; but Scott, recognising the horse-power in this fancy-gaited Pegasus and wanting to harness it to the *Guardian's* purposes, made Montague chief leader-writer. In Scott's eyes writing leaders for the *Guardian* was one of the highest functions a man could perform; it was not, however, what Montague most wanted to do. Would he have resigned his literary ambitions if he had known that some day he would be the *Guardian's* editor? At any rate he must have come finally to the realisation that he never would be.

His fellow writers on the *Guardian* staff looked on Montague with admiration and some envy. On the younger men particularly he was a risky literary influence. Howard Spring, recalling those days, says that "any man who worked there long was in danger of his life as a writer" because "the office was overrun with dangerous models. . . . C. E. Montague was the most dangerous of all." Yet it is hard to imagine that Montague's personal influence could have been anything but good. He was one of those shy men who radiate honesty and, in spite of melancholy, kindness. He might say little but he could encourage with a look. And he had what Scott had not—a sense of humour. He was the old soldier of the *Guardian.*

In 1914 he took leave from the *Guardian* to become a soldier in fact. At the age of 47 he enlisted as a private—with some difficulty because his prematurely white hair made him look even older. His one, quixotic idea was to get into action, but the Army disposed otherwise. He was promoted to Captain, put in Intelligence, and given the job of guiding distinguished visitors to the front lines. There at least he was often under fire, and won the rare reputation of actually enjoying it. Later he was put to censoring war correspondents' despatches. The war over, he returned to the *Guardian* and its leaders. He left the paper for good in 1925, planning to spend the rest of his life writing books. Three years later he died of pneumonia, at 61.

One reason, no doubt, that Scott did not consider Montague his proper successor was that the *Guardian* from its beginning had been a family heritage, handed down whenever possible from father to son. Scott intended his younger son Edward to succeed him; his other son, John, who had shown an interest in engineering, was schooled to be business manager. In 1913 Scott had divided the paper's Ordinary Shares equally between himself, his two sons and his son-in-law, Montague, and had drawn up an agreement that the share of any one of them who died or left the paper should be offered to the others.

It would have been difficult to measure the value of these shares. The *Guardian* was not losing money but it was no goldmine. After a decline in circulation of 13,000 caused by its opposition to the Boer War and perhaps even more by the competition of Manchester halfpenny papers, the circulation was slowly rising again, and in 1913 was nearly 50,000. Ten years later the *Guardian* began to buy shares of the Manchester *Evening News*, a sturdily successful money-maker, and by 1930 owned the *Evening News* outright. This gave the *Guardian* a very useful insurance against rainy days. But Scott was not interested in making money. Though as proprietor of the *Guardian* he could have pocketed all the profits, he used most of them to strengthen and improve the paper, but not to the extent of raising editorial salaries to Fleet Street level. He himself drew an annual salary never larger than £2,500.

When the old man finally prevailed on himself to retire, in 1929, he was happy in the knowledge that he had left the *Guardian* in good hands—hands he had trained himself. Edward Scott might have become as great an editor as his father; he had the education, the ability and the character; but time was not allowed to tell. For the first two years of his editorship he had to endure the shackling near-presence of the Editor-emeritus, trying not to interfere, imperfectly succeeding. Then, only a few months after C. P. Scott's death in 1931, Edward Scott was drowned in a boating accident on Windermere. The careful plans for the editorial succession thus tragically came to nothing. John Scott, the elder brother and business manager, was now the sole owner of the *Guardian*. He thereupon set up the Scott Trust, an arrangement which made permanent and mandatory the tradition his father had begun of taking no profits from the paper. The chief leader-writer, a scholarly, shy, peppery Oxonian named W. P. Crozier, was appointed Editor.

So great was the prestige the *Guardian* had built up under C. P. Scott and so strong was the momentum it had gathered that its Editor's sudden death caused an emergency but was not a catastrophe. The paper's personality had become more important than the personality of its Editor; the *Guardian* had long ceased to be—if in fact it had ever altogether been—a one-man affair, and could now be counted on to live by itself, attracting the kind of management and editorial staff its personality required. In the 13 years of Crozier's editorship the

Guardian's tone of voice remained as level as its circulation.

When Crozier died, in 1944, the *Guardian* was again faced with the necessity of picking a non-Scott as Editor. Though members of the Scott family and their Montague cousins held various positions on the paper, none was an obvious choice. But again the right man was ready to hand: Alfred Powell Wadsworth, the chief leader-writer. Scott had made the *Guardian* a great paper: Crozier had kept it going. Wadsworth developed it and made it better than ever.

Both as man and as editor, Wadsworth was a notable contrast to C. P. Scott. His background was humbler, his beginnings were harder. He was born in 1891 in Rochdale, near Manchester, where his father was a tailor. Though better informed and more deeply read than most university graduates, he had never been at a university He left school when he was 14, and that was the end of his formal education. He was an exceptionally bright boy, and had done so well at school that his grandfather offered to pay for his further schooling if he would become a Congregational minister. But the boy had other ideas. He went to work on the *Rochdale Observer*, learned shorthand ("with fury"), read everything he could lay his hands on, studied French and German, and worked at his job like a happy madman. He was never idle, even in church, where he sometimes sat in his grandfather's pew on Sundays, but took with him a Greek Testament and a lexicon to work at during dull sermons. At 15, besides his regular reporting, he was writing literary articles and studies of local history. When he was 16 he went alone to Germany for a fortnight's holiday, and the whole trip cost him £10.

After twelve years on the *Rochdale Observer* he joined the *Guardian*. One of his first assignments was in Ireland, reporting the villainies of the Black and Tans. His rise on the *Guardian* was steady (on any other paper it might have been spectacular), from reporter to special correspondent to leader-writer, ending up as Crozier's chief assistant. Wadsworth had been a journalist for 39 years when he became the Guardian's Editor. He had been cabin-boy, deck-hand, able seaman and chief engineer before he got his captain's papers. And he was a very different sort of captain from Scott, who had run the *Guardian* as a taut ship; under Wadsworth some grumblers said it was not taut enough—but nobody denied that it was a happy ship. A small, plump, soft-spoken, twinkling man, Wadsworth wore authority as if it were a rather threadbare joke—but he wore it, there was no doubt about that—and he hated fuss of any description.

Everyone had called C. P. Scott, to his face, "Mr. Scott"; most of his staff addressed Wadsworth as "A.P." Wadsworth was what Kipling called his old headmaster: "a downy bird". In fact he rather resembled a bird—an owl, perhaps, if an owl could look quizzical—but his perpetually raised eyebrows, that gave him an air of delighted amazement, and his padding walk also suggested a koala. He was quite evidently a man who got an inexhaustible amount of fun out of life: he sometimes managed to keep the fun to himself but he couldn't help showing it in his eyes. And yet the routine of his days appeared to be humdrum and hard. At home and at the office he worked long hours, six and often seven days a week, rarely went further afield than London and seldom took a holiday until illness forced it on him.

When he took over the *Guardian's* editorship he faced an emergency more acute than the one Crozier had had to meet. The second world war was still on, and it had wasted the staff to a skeleton, frozen the circulation and restricted paper. All he and his staff could do under these famine conditions was to tighten their belts and carry on as best they could, every man doing more than his share and Wadsworth more than any. The grinding weight of these years impaired his health and probably shortened his life. When peace came, and it was at last possible to do more than just hold on, he began to re-create the paper's foreign service and build up the staff both in London and Manchester. But the paper shortage continued, and he had to make the hard choice between giving up the *Guardian's* position as a great provincial newspaper or of abandoning its role as a national and international reporter—there was simply not enough paper to do both. He rightly decided to sacrifice his beloved Lancashire; the *Guardian's* personality had outgrown it.

Wadsworth served the *Guardian's* personality faithfully; though probably he would have denied it, he put his own mark on it too. He encouraged the light touch. Under his editorship the *Guardian's* style became more contemporary and colloquial than it had ever been. As James Bone, adding to Curzon, said: Scott made righteousness readable but Wadsworth also made it witty. The example of his unflagging ability was in the nature of a moral force and made itself felt as such, but there was nothing tyrannical about it. The fear human beings sometimes feel towards others of their kind is rooted in an actual doubt of their humanity; we often have to reassure ourselves that human beings are human. This wavering may be experienced not only about homicidal maniacs and the wartime enemy but about the boss in an office. Scott fostered that fear, whether he meant to or not; Wadsworth was a constant reassurance that the fear is unfounded.

He himself never aspired to speak with the tongues of angels, but considered that plain speech, pointed with mother-wit, would cover most human occasions. Of course you must also have something to say and know what you are talking about. Here, in his review of Beatrice Webb's diaries, is a characteristic example of his style:

> She was a rebel and a revolutionary but with a difference. She hated intellectual incompetence, was impatient of mediocrity, distrusted sentiment, detested demagogy. She was a Socialist but hardly a "comrade"; she despised the "Great Hearts with Weak Intellects", like Lansbury and A. J. Cook, and "the simple-minded and ignorant enthusiasts of the I.L.P. and the Clyde". And most trade unionists seemed dreadfully dim.

He applied the same easy manner to his conduct of the *Guardian.* The result, at times, looked like a mild attack of anarchy, but the inner reality was more orderly than the outward appearance. Sometimes he seemed to be practising masterly indecision: one of his staff would try to pin him down —"Do I go to Peru or not?" "Well," (softly, drifting away) "we'll have to see." (Nobody went to Peru.) On occasion he simply pocketed the problem and it disappeared for good. He didn't like the copy the advertising department had written for some advertisements promoting the *Guardian*; he thought them boastful. "Here, give them to me; *I'll* write you an ad," he said—and that was the end of them. His casualness was natural to him; it had some mischievousness in it; it was also the mark of his deep disdain of anything showy, "executive" or push-button.

One outright change he made in the paper's appearance seemed revolutionary at the time but in retrospect merely sensible. In 1952 he put news instead of advertisements on the front page, at the same time dropping the old Black Letter title for a roman heading designed by Eric Gill.

With all his mildness, he was a stubborn man. His friend and former teacher, Professor R. H. Tawney, speaks of his "enlightened pig-headedness absorbed from the complex of prejudices, habits, mental attitudes, style of life, work and thought native to the region in which his early years were passed; and whose characteristic blend of kindliness, remorseless realism and sardonic humour left its stamp on him for life." He could show temper too: when casualness went too far and something appeared in the *Guardian* that he didn't like and hadn't been shown, the guilty party was sure to receive a softly delivered but penetrating barb next day. When he was really angry he would sit looking down at his hands, saying nothing or muttering quietly to himself.

The occasions were made more impressive by their rarity. Most of the time Wadsworth was obviously enjoying himself. He was a past master at getting fun out of his job and had a quick eye for fresh opportunities. He would send the man in charge of book reviews to cover the Grace Kelly wedding in Monaco; he would give as much space to an archaeological find in the Middle East as to a change of government there; when the Alger Hiss trials in New York were being given the absent treatment by the rest of the press, he would run a full account nearly every day. And though anonymity cloaked nearly everything he wrote, his hand could be seen in such things as a letter to the *Guardian* (signed "A Student of the Press") joyfully listing the discrepancies in eight different newspaper accounts of the same event.

An outward and visible sign of his literary and scholarly appetite—and of his stubbornness—was his study. His office at the *Guardian*, where he spent his afternoons and evenings, came at least partly under the control of a neat-handed secretary, but his chaotic study at home was inviolate. Here, besides much of his work for the *Guardian*, he carried on his hobby, the pursuit of economic history. This was a passion with him. He was the joint author, with Dr. Julia Mann, of *The Cotton Trade and Industrial Lancashire*, a book which has been called the best history of an industry to be found in English. When he was working in London as Labour correspondent for the *Guardian*, before his day's work started he would drop in at the Record Office. Professor Tawney recalls those days: "To converse with him in the evening on his day's activities was to be treated to a mixed grill, in which hard-boiled, and sometimes sardonic, comments on the latest moves in coal, cotton and engineering were blended with reports of revelations wrung from the Chancery Proceedings and the State Papers Domestic."

Wadsworth's friends thought him exasperatingly modest about his scholarship. When he was offered an academic post at Oxford he turned it down because he said he had no qualifications for that kind of thing. And when the University of Manchester wanted to give him an honorary degree, "it was only after heated argument", said Tawney, "(in the course of which he was told that refusal would be an affront to his friends and to the university) that he was persuaded to accept." If circumstances had been different Wadsworth might have been a professor, and a famous one. And he might then have lived longer. For the strain of overwork, especially during the under-manned war years, sapped his health, which was never rugged, and brought on two severe illnesses. He never completely recovered from the second attack. In October, 1956, at the age of 64, he announced his retirement and the appointment of Alastair Hetherington as Editor. Four days later he was dead.

Wadsworth's term as Editor had been one of the shortest in the paper's history—only twelve years. Yet in that time the *Guardian's* circulation had more than doubled, from 70,000 to 170,000, and its reputation for being independent, liberal, humane and civilised was even more widely recognised than in C. P. Scott's day. To the momentum Scott had imparted to the *Guardian* Wadsworth had added a fresh impetus.

About his successor, Alastair Hetherington, little can be recorded yet but passport facts. A tall, sandy-haired, bespectacled Scot, with a solemn but cheerful manner, a slight burr and a great liking for his work, at the time of his appointment he was 36—the youngest Editor since C. P. Scott. He had been on the *Guardian* for only six years, specialising in foreign news and defence, and in that time had been promoted to leader-writer and made one of the three assistant editors. He came to the *Guardian* from the *Glasgow Herald* (Glasgow was his home and his father, Sir Hector Hetherington, is Vice-Chancellor of the University there); he had also worked on Hamburg's *Die Welt.* He had served six years in the Army during the war, chiefly in the Royal Armoured Corps, leaving with the rank of major. He was an Oxford man (at Scott's college, Corpus Christi) and had been a Commonwealth Fellow for a year at Princeton, in the U.S. He is a Presbyterian, newly married, and a near-teetotaller, but not gloomily or disapproving of those who hold other views. He had hardly seated himself in the Editor's chair when the Suez crisis burst upon him. The *Guardian* immediately labelled the Anglo-French intervention "an act of folly". A few days before, he had made the becomingly modest announcement that his aim would be "to carry on the paper in the same spirit as before. A better spirit could not be conceived."

Just before Wadsworth died, the *Guardian* printed two pages of tributes to him, mainly from fellow-journalists, many of whom knew him well. Taken together, these bits and pieces bore at least a sketchy likeness of the kind of man and editor he was: " . . . although he would disclaim it puncturingly, the tradition he hands on is his own . . . the *Guardian* has ideas without an ideology, principles without being doctrinaire, strong views without intolerance. . . . It is the mirror, in its virtues and its limitations alike, of the civilised—and impatient—common sense of the rare individualist who is now retiring . . . the demure appearance and vivid spark of intelligence . . . his skill in doing exactly what he wants to do by a process of deliberate indirection . . . you are debarred from saying what you think and feel about him. Before you start you can see the wicked gleam of eye, the slight twitch of the nostrils, with which he will devastate you for such sentimental nonsense, about him of all people. . . . I have never known a mind with a wider range or a quicker perception or a more unerring ability to detect pompousness, pretentiousness and sheer, plain silliness through the blanket of rhetoric in which, in England, these things are usually wrapped . . . his truly alarming memory. . . . Seldom can there have been a crusader whose armour was worn as lightly . . . an infinite relish for the fun as well as for the drama of public life . . . completely devoid of a sense of his own importance . . . the hardest, quickest and brightest worker in the office . . . utterly unlike the conventional idea of the 'great editor'—no drama, no grandiloquence, no heightening of issues . . . the most apparently casual of editors. He reduced organisation to the minimum: he had no liking for formal conferences or for fixed office hours. . . ."

These were public statements about a man still living, though he died only a few days later; nevertheless, not to be completely discounted: they have the generous ring of truth. And the truth they approximate is that Wadsworth was not only a first-rate editor but a lovable man. This was the great difference between him and C. P. Scott. Both were great editors and good men. But Wadsworth kindled more smiles of delight and attracted more affection.

A Mind of Its Own

In spite of its international standing, the *Manchester Guardian* is not listed as a "national" newspaper. This is because it is impossible to get a copy before breakfast in some parts of the United Kingdom, particularly in the regions south of London—in some places not before lunch and in others not at all. In short, the *Guardian* is not a national newspaper only because it cannot afford the machinery it would need for quicker distribution. In every sense but this technical one, the *Guardian* is a national paper: it is read throughout most of Britain and it is one of the few whose voice is heard abroad. Some day, when its milch cow, the Manchester *Evening News*, has made enough money, the *Guardian* may be able to print an edition in London, and thus become national in every sense.

The *Guardian* has a crowded branch office in London, but its headquarters and printing plant are in Manchester. Here, every night but Saturday, six editions of the paper are printed. This may seem an excessive number for a newspaper of comparatively small circulation, but the *Guardian's* readers are spread so widely through the country that these successive editions, sent on their way at different times during the night, are necessary. The London edition, the second, is timed to reach London at 4 a.m.—too late for early morning delivery much further south, too soon to include last-minute news of the night before. The final edition goes to press at 3 a.m. This is the one read in Manchester and its satellite towns, and may contain late news that never gets into the London edition.

Though the *Guardian* has ceased to be Manchester's favourite paper and its local circulation has fallen, it still has one foot firmly planted there. The *Guardian* building stands on Cross Street, in the heart of that ugly, smoke-grimed industrial capital of the Midlands. Built with mid-Victorian solidity of rough stone, its four floors that face Cross Street are occupied by the business offices and by the *Evening News*; behind this original pile an L-shaped addition of five storeys houses the *Guardian*, and the printing presses and bindery that serve both papers. Here the smell of ink and machinery is the same as in any newspaper plant, and when the presses are running the whole building's teeth chatter; but at other times the editorial offices are as quiet as a library.

In other respects too they resemble a library. The rooms have the high-ceilinged spaciousness still favoured by architects a generation or more ago. Many of them are wainscoted in dark wood and lined with glass book-cases. The library itself, of about 8,000 volumes, has spilled over into the conference room, along the editorial corridor and into the offices that open on it. In spite of this scatteration the books are arranged, catalogued and ticketed according to the best usages of the librarian's craft, for the *Guardian's* librarian, Geoffrey Whatmore, is a trained and certified professional. It pains him that he cannot completely control the incoming flow of periodicals: new journals often go direct to individual editors, who in principle pass them along to him when read, but they tend to forget.

The word "corridor" is used at the *Guardian* in a special sense and in inverted commas: it means the particular corridor where the Editor, his assistants and the other leader-writers have their offices—and thus has come to mean also the inner sanctum of the paper. Traditionally the doors of the "corridor" offices stand open. A closed door serves notice that the occupant is wrestling with a leader or has a visitor and doesn't want to be disturbed. The general air of settledness, of the unhurried passage of time, comes to a visual focus on the bulletin board outside the Editor's office. In Wadsworth's day it had a single notice, yellow with age, tacked on it:

FIRE!

Two fires have occurred recently owing to carelessness with matches or cigarette ends. Fortunately both were detected soon.

Great care should be exercised in the disposal of these.

22nd April, 1939 J. R. Scott.[1]

In the reporters' room the atmosphere is smoky with tradition but not so hushed; it is no bear-garden either. According to an office story, perhaps apocryphal: when Neville Cardus, now a fine old crusty vintage of a *Guardian* writer, was one of the boys there, he once cut his two weeks' holiday short because he got homesick for the talk in the reporters' room.

Across the corridor from the Editor's office is the conference room, as stiff and un-used-looking as a front parlour: besides the ever-present bookcases along three sides of its walls, it contains a forbiddingly long table with chairs set around it. Here at 6.15 every afternoon the Editor and eight or ten others assemble: assistant editors, leader-writers, night editor, news editor, chief sub-editor, foreign sub-editor, the picture man. Everyone brings a typed copy of the items reported on the 6 o'clock B.B.C. News ("M. Faure and Dr. Adenauer have agreed that result of Saar referendum must not upset relation between two governments. . . . Syrian troops reported to have opened fire on Israel settlement. . . . Head of Hitler's SS Division released from prison") and a two-page typed list of the news, articles and leaders tentatively scheduled for next day's paper.

This agenda looks impressive but it is not treated impressively. Wadsworth never let the performance run longer than 15 minutes. Both eyebrows resignedly raised, and one at times rising impossibly higher, he would run his pencil down the list, murmuring as if to himself: "Hmm. Zinkin still not in? Hmm.

[1] The notice is still there, but has now been joined by others.

What's this mean? Myxo——. Oh, myxomatosis. What an awful word. Mmm. How long will the Parliamentary report run? Better hold most of the second page, I suppose. Well, well. Mmm. Lisbon earthquake? Surely that was years ago. Eighteenth century? A bit old even for us, isn't it? 'Bootle student and girl found dead.' Hmm. Well, what about pictures?" The night editor has brought the dummy with him, and there is a sketchy discussion about the position of the Sports page, how much space for pictures (never very much), whether So-&-So's piece couldn't be held over yet *another* day . . . The Editor says a final "Well . . . ", pushes the list away from him, and the conference breaks up.

Wadsworth's attitude towards this daily ritual seemed to say that it was mildly amusing, slightly vexatious, unimportant, a brief interruption of the day's work, like a coffee break. He presided over it lightly and obliquely, almost as if he were trying to create the impression that he was helplessly out of touch with these formidable but rather boring realities. Any of the other editors, if questioned about the conference, would say promptly, "It's a farce." For in fact, of course, it was understood that Wadsworth had all the essentials of the forthcoming paper in his head and refused to be bothered with pesky details—or, if that was putting it a little too neatly, that he knew from long experience enough of the ingredients were there to ensure the mixture as before. It is traditional among the *Guardian* staff to assume an air of faint surprise that the paper has once again managed to get itself out. Partly in pride, partly in humorous deprecation, they would agree with the *Guardian* graduate who called it "the most easy-going newspaper in the world". It is the common British form of boasting by belittling oneself, or pretending to.

Wadsworth, himself one of the most deprecating of men, was nevertheless outspokenly proud of the *Guardian* for being easy-going—in the sense of letting a writer have his head, if he had a good head. He once wrote: "No daily paper, perhaps, ever gave greater freedom to the individual play of the minds of its staff or permitted them more idiosyncrasy in the handling of their material: it is a precious tradition which the *Guardian* has always valued." The tradition was established by C. P. Scott, but Wadsworth encouraged and developed it. There is no conscious training of *Guardian* reporters: they are sent to find out about something and report it as well as they can. The News Editor, W. E. Cockburn, who is in charge of the reporters in the Manchester office, says: "We're always delighted when they write in their own way." Needless to say, this encouraging latitude does not imply continuing delight if their work fails to measure up to the *Guardian's* standard. Most men who come to work for the paper have had some previous experience, but the *Guardian* will often take on a youngster who has had none, if he seems promising. And some recruits are specialists with no training in journalism; the present science writer, for example, had been a teacher of physics. When the *Guardian* sent him to Leningrad with a British naval squadron, instead of reporting or even attending the official ceremonies, he met a Russian girl named Olga and wrote about her instead. The articles were a great success.

Though Manchester is the *Guardian's* headquarters, London is its front line. Of the eighty-odd members of the editorial staff, some 25 work in London, and several of these are specialists who deal directly with Manchester. The remaining baker's dozen, under the direction of the London Editor, Gerard Fay, have their hands full. One way or another the London office supplies a third to a half of the paper's regular contents: the London letter, Parliamentary and Diplomatic correspondence, financial news, general news, reviews of West End plays, cinemas, ballet, art, special articles and occasional leaders. The London office, crowded into a small building in Fleet Street, has twice the bustle and urgency of Manchester.

The *Guardian* has no Sunday edition, but since 1919 it has printed a 16-page weekly anthology of its best bits. This *Weekly* (price 4*d.*) has a circulation of about 40,000—half of it overseas. The daily *Guardian* costs 3*d.* and is made up of a basic

12 to 14 pages, with occasional supplementary pages on special subjects. The page size is 17·5 by 25 in.—the traditionally generous, old-fashioned newspaper size—divided into seven columns, except in the classified advertisement pages, which have eight. Throughout the paper the typography and layout are sober, conservative and graceless. The *Guardian* does not spend much time thinking about its appearance.

The headlines are informative, uninviting statements at the opposite extreme from the *Mirror's* editorial yells. This is a typical front-page two-column head:

MAJOR CONCESSIONS
TO SINGAPORE
Modifications of Governor's
Powers
MR. MARSHALL'S VICTORY

Guardian headlines are so cautious, indeed, that they often show a tendency to appear in question form. In one issue (October 22, 1955) four of the six leaders were headed: *France to the Polls?, More on the Bottle?, Aiders and Abetters?, Mild or Bitter?*

The main news is carried on the first page—a revolutionary change made by Wadsworth that has been in force only since 1952; the first page used to be solid notices and advertisements, as it was, is and ever shall be in the London *Times*. Turn the page and the *Guardian* becomes more recognisably itself. The inside of the paper is a medley, arranged according to a traditional order, of news, Miscellany, fiction, book-reviews, Country Diary, letters to the editor, sport, Low's cartoon, *causeries* on motoring, music, women's clothes, food, the cotton market, etc., etc. The *Guardian* is made up half of news and half of something else. The "something else"—comment, descriptions, criticism or narrative—is valued highly by *Guardian* readers, perhaps even more highly by the men who write it. It may be doubted whether the leaders, for example, are read as conscientiously as they are written, or indeed whether they are read regularly and thoroughly by most *Guardian* readers. Nevertheless, the political leaders, at any rate, are scrutinised by editors of other papers and often quoted by them.

Whichever section of the paper is in fact the most important, it is not the *Guardian's* news columns that have won it the name of a great paper. If a newspaper is to be judged solely on the promptness, completeness and accuracy with which it reports the news, can the *Guardian* even be considered a good newspaper? It has been called "a wonderful newspaper about the day before yesterday", the implication being that the *Guardian* is too slow on the draw, and a bit too easy-going and old-fashioned altogether. This exaggeration has some basis in fact. Besides the handicap of its being printed in Manchester and thus being unable to get late-breaking news into its London edition, the *Guardian* actually prefers to use a great deal of its space for fuller and more leisurely reports than many other papers would make, and also for a kind of Third Programme material which is certainly not yesterday's news. On the other hand, in some important areas—notably news from America—the *Guardian* gives fuller coverage than any paper in Britain. The answer to the question of how good a newspaper the *Guardian* is depends on what you mean by "newspaper". Is a newspaper's quality to be judged by the number of its news items? The *Daily Telegraph*, for example, prints many more news items every day than the *Guardian* does. But if the quality of a newspaper is to be measured by the comprehensiveness—and comprehension—of its report on the world, then the *Guardian* is a far better paper than the *Telegraph*.

Anonymity was once the invariable rule in journalism. It is so no longer, and the *Guardian* now follows much the same illogical practices that have spread through most of the Press. Its leaders and most news despatches are unsigned. Some reports —e.g., Parliamentary, Foreign and City—are signed not by the writer's name but by a title: our special Correspondent (here a name is sometimes added, more often not), our own Correspondent, our Correspondent (only the *Guardian* knows or cares about the fine shade of distinction between these two), our Parliamentary Correspondent, our Diplomatic Correspondent, our Industrial Staff, our Parliamentary Staff, our Financial Editor. Other items—A Country Diary, some reviews of books, plays, art shows, etc.—are initialled. And at least ten or twelve despatches a day are signed with the writer's name: most of the American correspondence, special articles, many reports on sport, short stories, and the star turns of the chief reporter, Norman Shrapnel.

This complicated system of masks, half-masks and dominoes is not carried on from any need or desire for secrecy: it is traditional, the relic of a simpler age when the cult of individual personality had not yet become the established faith and men were more content to serve a master. Its continuance, even in this muddled form, bears witness to the journalist's belief that a newspaper's personality is all-important, and that the men who preserve and enhance it must always be subordinate to it.

The *Guardian's* personality is as distinct and recognisable as the *Mirror's*, but quieter and more complex: the *Guardian* is older, better educated, and more aware of itself—especially of the writers who have made it and who make it what it is. It is naturally more self-conscious, in the sense of being more self-critical. With Wadsworth's amused blessing—he referred to it as an "inquiry from another planet"—I circulated a questionnaire among the editorial staff about their attitude to the *Guardian*. One of the questions was: "Can you put the *Guardian's* tone of voice into a sentence or two—as if you were quoting a characteristic remark of a real person?" These were some of the answers:

> "Its potential circulation is limitless but only in as much as the *Guardian* is the newspaper of the intelligent student and further education is becoming increasingly available; its potential circulation is limited in as much as the number of people with sufficient intelligence to benefit from further education is necessarily restricted."

"He's right up to a point, but of course there's more to it than that."

"(At its best): 'In fairness it must be said . . .'

(At its worst): 'It depends what you mean by "niggle". . . . ' "

"Thank you, Sir Anthony; the bishopric would be nice, but we'd rather not wear gaiters."

"There's another side to this, you know."

"Surely no sane person could think this is the best way to go about an admittedly difficult problem."

"After all, performing animals have their rights."

"Of course I've got ideals, but when you get to my age . . ."

"Nothing that glitters is gold. Every silver lining has its dirty cloud. Read the *Manchester Guardian* and get that smile off your face."

"It seems best to exclude from mass destruction all towns and cities over a certain size, except . . . "[1]

"It's not half as bad as you say but I agree that it should be stamped out. Not for the reasons you give, though, but because it's wasteful, impracticable, silly, not a bit funny and unjust."

Does a tone of voice emerge? I think it does; and some undertones as well. Is it perhaps just a little superior? Not smug, no; not self-righteous—oh, no. But very faintly irritating all the same?—the patiently didactic, smiling voice of the bluestocking. Not laying down the law but lecturing on it.

The *Guardian's* tone of voice is heard most distinctly, of course, in its leader page. As its Washington correspondent, Max Freedman, once told a meeting of American editorial writers: "Every national newspaper in England . . . competes at once for the attention of the public mind. Under these circumstances there must be far less emphasis on local news, and the editorial debate must grapple with the themes that engage and dominate

[1] Quoted from a *Guardian* leader.

the national mind. As a result there is a fierce stress of competition between the editorial pages of Great Britain, a pride in intellectual leadership and in the swift impact on public policy, quite unknown in the American Press." Whatever the fact of the matter may be, the *Guardian* takes it for granted that its leaders are widely read, pondered and discussed, and in consequence regards the leader page as the core of the paper. Here the *Guardian* speaks its mind.

Is it a good mind? Its readers, many of whom are intellectuals, most of whom are well enough educated to look down on the less-well-educated, would agree that it is. An ambiguous admirer has called it "the best mind in England—until it's made up". The Guardian has always had a mind of its own, and is justly proud of its long record of dissent. The paper has never truckled to public opinion nor to the opinions of its readers. Its convictions it acquired long ago, in C. P. Scott's day. A strong upholder of the unwritten form of constitution and a disbeliever in creeds and slogans, the *Guardian* has fought shy of formally stating those convictions. A former London Editor, James Bone, asked to say what he thought was the paper's guiding aim, replied after an oracular pause: "Always think of it but never speak of it". On occasion, however, the *Guardian* has "spoken of it", at least to the extent of making or approving a general statement which would seem to fit an unwritten credo. C. P. Scott announced the first two of the following, and all four are implicit in the tradition he left to the paper:

"*Comment is free but facts are sacred.*"
"*A newspaper is a public institution.*"
Patriotism is not enough.
Moral force is the only effective force.

If a newspaper (which means the men who write, edit and publish it) believes such statements to be true, then we should expect it to be as out of place in the modern world as a minor prophet among stockbrokers. For although the public at large —and the popular Press that caters to it—pays lip service to the first two of those beliefs, it really qualifies them into something like this:

Comment is propaganda and facts are counters in a game.
A newspaper is a valuable private property.
Patriotism is more than enough.
Physical force is the only effective force.

Scott made righteousness readable, and to a great extent Scott's spirit still infuses the *Guardian*. But, as it was never altogether his paper, so there have always been members of the staff who were more concerned about the question of manner than the question of morals. It might almost be said of the *Guardian* as a whole that righteousness and readability struggle for the upper hand. In the leader page there is no question which has the mastery. There it is argument on a high level, and the style is plain, unadorned, lucid, the opposite of stylish. The leaders are emotionally quiet too: a cool, impersonal hand laid on the feverish problems of economic and political evil. "Feel deeply, think clearly, and hold yourself in." It is the attitude of the rational humanist who contends that right is always legible or can be made so—for the man with eyes sufficiently well-trained to read it. In common with the vast majority of "decent, godless people" who make up the so-called Christian world, the *Guardian* is humanist, not religious; but it champions decency and godlessness with the earnestness of faith.

As Scott and his forebears dissented from the Established Church, so the *Guardian* has dissented from the secular Establishment—the entrenched position of "the best people". Some of its lost causes, like woman's suffrage, were finally won. Others, like its opposition to the Boer War, were hopeless from the start. It is all one to the *Guardian*, which would rather be right than be read, as long as there are enough readers to keep it going—and there always have been, though at times just barely. The

Guardian has never held with political rain-making nor believed that such interfering miracles, which it also regards as somewhat fishy, are the right way to tackle the endless problem of reclaiming the human Waste Land. Its own modest method is not to beat the drums for rain but to argue the advantages of irrigation.

The *Guardian's* relations with its little band of 170,000 readers are as characteristically cool as the Mirror's relations with its 5,000,000 are warm. *Mirror* readers are treated like members of a huge, brawling family; *Guardian* readers like fellow-citizens. The *Guardian* doesn't know very much about them except by putting two and two of them together in the Correspondence columns, and would regard it as an invasion of their privacy as well as a waste of its time to try to find out much more. In 1951, however, the *Guardian* was curious enough to have a survey made which disclosed one or two interesting facts: that in the preceding twelve years the paper had gained many more men than women as new readers; and that less than half its middle-aged readers, and only a quarter of the younger, said they read the whole paper.

No readership test has been necessary to conclude that a great part of the *Guardian's* readers are members of the intelligentsia. By *Oxford Dictionary* definition, obviously written by a member of the club, that means: "the class consisting of the educated portion of the population and regarded as capable of forming public opinion". A more up-to-date way of putting it, perhaps, would be: "the people who listen to the Third Programme and whose social and political views are liberal". They are likely to be middle-class, middle-aged, middle-income and—in the American phrase—upper-middle-brow.

If the *Guardian* has a conscious purpose and it could be simply stated, it might be put something like this: to keep reminding its readers that civilisation exists and is worth preserving. To do that with any effectiveness, the *Guardian* itself must be both an exponent and an example of the civilisation it upholds. Though its own staff is critical of the paper's performance—none more so—they all agree that the *Guardian* is essentially a civilised newspaper. They are proud to be working on it.

The Men behind the Guardian

A newspaper is one of the flimsiest things man ever made—not a bit like the Pyramids. And journalists take a sardonic satisfaction in reminding one another of the fact. They say: "as dead as yesterday's paper", or "you can always use yesterday's paper to wrap fish in". Every day a newspaper has to be re-created, and though it avails itself wherever it can of machinery and mass-production methods, essentially it is hand-made. Its existence depends on the daily renewed efforts of the men who write it.

Equally, an established newspaper, one with a known and welcome personality, may be more toughly continuous than the human beings who produce it, and vital enough to outlive them and their generation as well. The present personality of the *Daily Mirror*, which was ripped into being, as it were, by Caesarean operation, is barely 20 years old; the *Guardian's* personality has matured slowly over 136 years. The men behind the *Guardian* go back in a long perspective.

C. P. Scott is still the great father-figure, the household god whose presiding image hardly needs the added reminders of Epstein's flamboyant bust or the photographs of his fierce, handsome old man's bearded face glaring down from office walls. And though his dream of a dynasty failed, it did not come to nothing: there are still "founder's kin" in high places at the *Guardian*. Laurence Prestwich Scott, a grandson, is Chairman of the company and Managing Director of the paper; his cousin, Richard Scott, another grandson, is Diplomatic Correspondent. A third grandson, Larry Montague, son of C. E., is Sports Editor (an elder brother, now dead, was London Editor). There are descendants of other *Guardian* names too: Monkhouse, Arnold, Bone.

Laurence Scott, whose position at the *Guardian* is comparable to Cecil King's at the *Mirror*, is a tall, good-looking, young-middle-aged man with slightly protuberant eyes, sensitive mouth, and a firm jaw. He has a look of eagerness—borne out in conversation—and his manner is cordial if somewhat formal. In sum he gives the impression of a controlled idealist, acquainted with the wiles of Mammon and thus armed against them, who knows that a balanced budget is a primary moral duty. Compared to King's his journalistic ambitions are so modest and impersonal as to be almost non-existent: he wants the *Guardian* to grow and prosper as a worthy public institution, and believes it will. Power, in King's sense, in the way the Press lords dream of it, is beneath his ken.

In appearance, his cousin Larry Montague is more obviously a chip off the old block. He has the same long Irish upper lip as his father, the same generous mouth, premature white hair, the large and patient ears. He is stocky and thickly-knit, and walks with the slight forward stoop of the rugger player he once was. But Scott blood has fired him: he is quick of speech, receptive of company, his face limbers up with enthusiasm. His manner is courteous to a degree now a little old-fashioned. He seemed an odd fit for a sports editor, until you heard him talking on his subject, or read what he wrote. He is a scholar and a student of games. All sports editors tend to be autonomous, but Larry Montague was more autonomous than most. He was king of his page on the *Guardian*, and he and his eight-man staff filled it in princely style.[1] He has never tried to imitate his father—C. E. Montague has no followers now—but writes like a serious and straightforward professional, a reassuringly sensible tone among the brummagem and bombast of the ordinary sports page. This, from an unsigned leader on the retirement of Len Hutton, England's cricket captain, is the sort of thing he and his staff turn out:

> Mr. Hutton's captaincy, like his batsmanship, was exceptional in kind. It was, so to say, highly professional captaincy;

[1] No longer Sports Editor, Montague has been made a director and an assistant editor.

lacking something in dash, in inspiration or even imagination; but infinitely knowledgeable, resourceful, and prudent, so that (with the disastrous exception of the Brisbane Test) his errors gave very little away, and his successful strokes were relentlessly pressed home. It was not a method to make for easy popularity; yet he was a popular captain, too. His own integrity and personal modesty and Yorkshire humour shone through the chain mail which he put on for the battle, and won him friends as well as matches.

Traditionally, the hardest-working man on any paper is the Editor, and Alastair Hetherington is not the man to let that tradition down. Yet the duties of an editor call for frequent interruptions which make it impossible for him to settle down for long periods into a steady work-horse pace. On the *Guardian* the brunt of this heavy ploughing and harrowing falls on the shoulders of two assistant editors: P. J. Monkhouse and J. R. L. Anderson. Monkhouse, who is also Deputy Editor, is the elder by ten years; he is in his early fifties. Both men look much older than their age.

Born near Manchester, Monkhouse was brought up in the august shadow of the *Guardian*, where his father made his career as a writer under C. P. Scott. Apparently one has to be a native to feel affection for the city or even to like it (Monkhouse does both); latecomers rarely become acclimatised. *Guardian* men who are non-Mancunians will tell you: "Oh, it's an awful place. There isn't any good hotel. The intellectual life of the city? Not what it used to be. Nobody would live here if they didn't have to." But Monkhouse is strongly in favour of his native town. The grimy streets and hideous buildings roll off his retina; what he sees are its shrewd and sturdy qualities, its humanitarian habits. From his almost non-existent spare time he snatches a day off to serve his city (without pay) as a local magistrate. He has the homely, rugged, broad Mancunian face; his hair too has turned white before its time, and his eyes blink and twitch from overwork. His voice, slightly hoarse, has a note of anxious kindliness. His speciality is writing leaders on the arts and on colonial affairs, but he can turn his hand to any journalistic problem. Shortly after taking his degree at Oxford he came to the *Guardian* and, with a lapse of several years on Beaverbrook's *Evening Standard*, has been there ever since.

His junior colleague, John Anderson, who specialises in leaders on home affairs, especially Labour and economics, looks like a don who is nearly at the end of his tether. But his appearance belies him: he is sardonic rather than donnish. Of middle height and slightly built, he has deep-set eyes, close together; from either side of a longish nose two incised lines run down to the corners of his lips. Behind this frowning front is a startling generosity of wit and feeling. He stares at the floor, heaves a sigh and says, at right angles to the conversation, "Do you like cats?" (What he means is: "Why not leave that ratty hotel and stay at my house?")

Anderson is not acclimatised to Manchester: his birthplace was far away, in British Guiana. Sent to school in England, he afterwards worked on a weekly paper near London (the £1-a-week pay helped acclimatise him to the rewards of "quality" journalism in Britain), and did some correspondence for the *Guardian*. The war took him away for five years, as a captain in the Royal Garhwal Rifles. He was invalided home in 1944, and became a *Guardian* war correspondent in France, then Berlin correspondent. He was called back to London the following year to become Labour Correspondent, and was later made one of the assistant editors in Manchester.

In any list of the men who make the *Guardian* what it is, the name of Norman Shrapnel must come near the top. On a less dignified paper he would be known as the star reporter. In his case, journalist and writer mean the same first-rate thing. Like C. E. Montague before him, he is the admired stylist of the *Guardian* staff, and worth emulating. He works in and from Manchester, with the majority (14) of the paper's reporters, but his assignments may take him anywhere in Britain or abroad. And they may be almost anything: the Caledonian Games, an investigation of the high suicide rate in a Midlands town, dog-racing in the Lakes, a performance of *Elizabeth of England* in Ljubljana, the revival of an early Oscar Wilde melodrama at the University of Durham, a show of fancy mice at Bradford, a review of Evelyn Waugh's latest novel. This is the kind of reporting he does:

> She may be only a poor weak woman, but she has the heart of a partisan, the passion of a Bernhardt, the thoroughgoing technique of a professor of acting—which, indeed, is what she is in the hours (they appear to be few) she can be spared from the Slovene National Theatre in Ljubljana. One's admiration rides high; the danger—Yugoslav hospitality demanding at least the return of courtesy—is of dislocating one's jaw in stifling monumental yawns. It is hard to realise how far we in Britain have got away from the high school of academic acting. . . . .
>
> The fancy mouse, it seems, sometimes likes to gnaw whiskers: not its own, in the way that people gnaw their finger-nails, but those of others. A rogue mouse will occasionally be seen sitting in a corner, looking inordinately bright-eyed and fulfilled, and all the other occupants of the box will have lost their whiskers. The rogue has eaten them. . . .
>
> The set-piece of blazing London with which *Officers and Gentlemen* opens has a fierce gaiety that could have come from no other pen now at work; it is merry as the night is long, and as funny as hell. . . .

Few reporters write like that, or could—even if they were allowed to try. And on what paper but the *Guardian* would they be encouraged to try? The *Guardian* still holds with the old-fashioned principle (which is now, says its London Editor, Gerard Fay, regarded as revolutionary) "that a qualified reporter knows best—that he can be trusted to write accurately, knowledgeably and at the proper length on his assignment." Fay has been a reporter himself, and knows what he means by "qualified". Shrapnel certainly is. So, presumably, are the five reporters who work under Fay's eye in London. One came to the paper with even broader qualifications than a Balliol Scholar's: among other things he had been a Guards officer, a Church of England parson, a Covent Garden porter.[1]

The *Guardian's* London office jumps and quivers with life on its own account; it also houses half a dozen specialists who deal directly with Manchester. The paper's famous New-Zealand-born cartoonist Low, once the Great Auk of Beaverbrook's *Daily Express*, lives in London but rarely visits the office; he sends in his cartoons four times a week. Here too is an autonomous department: the City office (London financial news) under the Financial Editor, Richard Fry, with a staff of three men. But the man-in-charge in London, who is supposed to know what everybody is doing, whether it is being done, where everyone is and why, is Gerard Fay, the London Editor. He is in effect a managing editor with the additional duties of an office manager who also writes whenever his continual interruptions allow him.

Anyone who expects a *Guardian* editor to look like a diplomat or a schoolmaster might be surprised at first sight of Gerard Fay in his cheerful Tattersall waistcoat and bow tie. A cool Irishman, of middle height, in his early 40's, he has what Americans call a deadpan face; and he speaks in a monotone: "Why not? Yes, I'll see to that. We expect him this afternoon. About 4." Unless he is closeted with an urgent problem, his office door is always open; he is used to being barged in on and doesn't mind, or at any rate can stand it. If you hesitate in the doorway, seeing him attached to the telephone or another visitor, he waves his hand brusquely downward, indicating the sofa. It is a gesture of welcome without formalities. But the best place to get his ear is in a slack half-hour at El Vino, over a glass of

[1] British journalism is as much—or more—a man's world as Britain is. There are a few women on its editorial staff: including Jenny Nasmyth; Nesta Roberts, Deputy News Editor; Mrs. Mary McManus, writer on television and radio; and Mrs. E. T. Roberts and Miss Adrienne Keith-Cohen, sub-editors in the London office.

Chablis. There you can talk to him, but not chat. He is a man preoccupied and content.

His father, Frank Fay, was one of the founders of Dublin's once-famous Abbey Theatre. Dublin was his home till he was 17, and he went to school there. His first paper was the same as Wadsworth's, the *Rochdale Observer*. The *Guardian* took him on just before the war; then the Army received him for the usual five years. He was a major in the South Wales Borderers, and was badly wounded in France in August 1944. Back on the *Guardian* at last, he went from reporter to leader-writer to the London office, and became London Editor in 1955. Like Wadsworth, he runs a happy ship.

Next to Fay, the other key executive (but he also writes; everybody writes on the *Guardian*) is Richard Fry, the Financial Editor. His ramrod straightness and slight German accent are accounted for by the fact that he was born in Germany; he changed his name from Freund. Perhaps that also explains why he does not altogether agree with the *Guardian's* policy of giving reporters their heads, right from the start, and insists on a certain background and training for all his young writers. Financial reporters, of course, have to be specialists in a toughly technical field. His staff all have university degrees in economics —that is Fry's first requisite—and they must also relax their pens and clear their vocabularies of economic cant by reading Gibbon's *Autobiography* and Kipling's *Kim*. A surprising combination, it may be thought; but Fry swears by it. The daily financial page that he and his Gibbonian-Kiplingites get out is only half the size of the *Times's*, but in Fry's opinion—and solid men in the Manchester cotton market and in the City of London agree with him—it is packed with quite as much useful information and its comment carries at least as much weight. The real competition, in Fry's view, is with the City's leading paper, the *Financial Times*.

Then there are the specialists. They are not by any means one-note men. Nor are they, all of them, eccentrics, though there is a dash of eccentricity in most. Take the oldest and perhaps most valued of the lot: the veteran Parliamentary Correspondent, Harry Boardman. He "reports" Parliament—which is to say that he writes about it as the spirit moves him, with irony, hilarity, affection and long knowledge; it is his favourite club and he one of its oldest members. He reports its doings, its carryings-on, its temper with the privilege and the insight of an old, old hand. His accounts of Parliament could not possibly be confused with "straight" reporting; how much better, livelier, more illuminating, truer they are than that! Here are some excerpts from a recent "report" of his, really an unabashed defence of "The Vitality of the Commons":

> . . . Parliament believes in itself, which is something of a virtue at this moment. The cynical will reply that the tanner always believes there is nothing like leather. But let anyone on any day spend a few hours in the House of Commons, not omitting if possible question hour, and if he is fully alive himself and free from dyspepsia he will have no doubts about its virility. . . .
>
> There will always be those who, thinking with their livers or being elderly and the survivors, as they consider themselves, of a golden age, will decide that it is all over with Parliament. Dickens wrote to Forster in 1855: 'I really am serious in thinking that representative government is become just the dreariest failure and nuisance that ever bothered this much-bothered world.' Carlyle thought the House of Commons the best proof of the existence of the devil. He should have lived to attend a meeting of the Congress of Soviets when Stalin was in full cultivation of his personality . . . The end appeared really at hand on the famous Irish night, compared with which the Suez turbulence pales. Were not the Irish members carried out of the Chamber, each with a policeman holding him by the head and the feet? And was not the melting appeal heard from one, Mr. Flanagan, 'Go aisy with me b'hoys' as his posterior kept striking the floor? . . .

The *Guardian's* foreign staff is small but very select, and their despatches are prominently displayed in the paper's shop-window. The most constant eye-catcher is the American correspondence, and the by-line most frequently attached to it is Alistair Cooke's. He is the fair-haired boy of the *Guardian*, with editors and readers alike. And this might seem odd, for while Fay doesn't look like the popular notion of a *Guardian* man, Cooke doesn't sound like one. Sprightliness, the gay and knowing wink, the feather touch are his speciality. The heavy weights he has to lift (reports of UNO meetings, for example) sometimes slow him to the tempo of an adagio dancer, but even then he will kid the act when he gets a chance, and whenever he can, which is nearly always, he turns the job into a light-hearted juggling act, with grins and wisecracks thrown in. At his best he is brilliant, at his least he is light. A chimpanzee on the loose in New York is just his dish:

> For ten hours yesterday an escaped chimpanzee, refusing to answer to the name of Mike, cantered across the roof tops of the Lower East Side and alternately amused and terrified a great crowd standing in the rain. New York has enjoyed no such prolonged defiance by the animal kingdom since King Kong held Fay Wray in the palm of his hand and clawed the United States Air Force from the mast on top of the Empire State building. . . .
>
> First, they [the cops] heaped a little mound of doped bananas and etherised oranges by way of inviting Mike to lunch. He swiped them all, went back on the rostrum and beat his breast, in the usual chimp fashion of asking for more. As dusk came on they fell back, in the classic "Scarface" fashion, on tear gas and ammonia. Trapped gangsters always succumb to these smelling salts and invariably end up crying for their mothers. But, unlike the nets and nooses, they require for their maximum efficacy a rising column of air. It was raining heavily yesterday and the fumes tended to condense into knock-out drops and descend to knock out the cops.

> This is the only satisfactory explanation of why it took another six hours to catch Mike once he was trapped. . . .
>
> At one time the despairing cops granted the plea of George Zenkewich, an S.P.C.A. agent, to let him use his expert charm on the beast. Mr. Zenkewich went on the roof after him and came close enough to show he was fearless and unarmed. Mr. Zenkewich extended a helping arm, and Mike bit it. Mr. Zenkewich was never so sore in all his life. He was rushed off for first aid. . . .

Cooke's light-heartedness sometimes gets him into trouble. In a series of serious reports, later re-published in pamphlet form, on how the South was responding to the Supreme Court ruling against segregation, he gave an eyewitness account (he was the only white reporter there) of a Negro meeting in Montgomery, Alabama:

> Now we were to hear from the Rev. King, an educated man. This great movement had started, he said, "without the external and internal attachments in terms of organisational structure". They listened in awe. If they or their children came to be "integrated" they, too, could get to write like this. The Rev. King was indeed a master of Pentagon, or Federal, prose. . . .

The minute this despatch reached America he was hotly attacked by the National Association for the Advancement of Coloured People for being "anti-Negro". The series as a whole, and Cooke's record, made nonsense of this charge; but about sacred subjects and on holy ground you simply must not laugh.

Alistair Cooke, however, like the late H. L. Mencken, as an American (by adoption) naturally spends most of his time laughing. One reason he finds the United States inextinguishably amusing is that he is in love with the country, in a way that perhaps only a converted Britisher can be. He was a Lancashire boy who got away early and went to New York to seek a better fortune. He found an embarrassment of riches: broadcasting for the B.B.C. (he put on the first "jam session" ever broadcast, and now does a weekly "Letter from America"); compering a TV show, *Omnibus*; and covering the entire nation —except Washington—for the *Guardian*. On this enormous assignment he has seen more of America than any American reporter, and prides himself on knowing the country better. Thanks to him the *Guardian* gave a much fuller account of the Alger Hiss trials than any British paper, and most American.

And thanks to his account of the evangelist Billy Graham, doing his stuff in New York's Madison Square Garden, the *Guardian* drew such a bombardment of letters, pro and con, as the editors had rarely seen:

> What is modern and superior in [Billy Graham's] cunning, and it could be wholly unconscious, is the prohibition of all applause. He cages up his audience for thirty minutes and dangles red meat from outside. And when he finally braces his splendid biceps and bends the bars apart, where else can the sprung prisoners go but to him? . . .

If it were possible to name the most generally popular feature in the *Guardian*, a likely choice would be Alistair Cooke's despatches. And yet this laughing cavalier (would C. P. Scott altogether have approved of him?) does not quite seem to fit the generally Roundhead tradition of the *Guardian*; he remains something of an anomaly, a significant oddity. Cooke's colleague, Max Freedman, who has been the paper's Washington correspondent for the past several years, more nearly fits the orthodox likeness of a *Guardian* writer. Sometimes, indeed, the fit is almost uncomfortably tight. Freedman comes from Canada, and has kept his Canadian citizenship, but gives the impression of even more distant origins—say, the late eighteenth or early nineteenth century. Though he is capable of Johnsonian irony and Landorian eloquence, he is never light, either of mind or heart. In fact, he is sometimes pretty heavy: "It is only against the ennobling perspective of its later glory that the publication of *Leaves of Grass* takes on the dimensions of a notable event in the history of literature." But his heaviness has also an armour-piercing quality, as may be seen in these further remarks on Walt Whitman's centenary:

> There was always Carlyle, for example, to growl that Whitman was the parish bull with a pen in his hand. One must remember, as Sir Walter Raleigh remarked, that a certain exercise of contempt was necessary to Carlyle's mind to keep it in health. . . . When one thinks of the indignation and fury that have constantly flashed round Whitman's name one can only echo the wisdom of Dr. Johnson and repeat that there are some outrages which seem to be ebullitions of minds agitated by stronger resentment than bad poetry can excite. . . .
>
> Among many towering virtues and some garish blunders [Whitman] is worth remembering on this centenary if only for his immortal warning against the never-ending audacity of elected persons.

Freedman's hobby, and the labour of his spare hours, is the study of the United States Supreme Court. C. P. Scott would certainly have approved of *him*.

In one of William Saroyan's freely wandering plays, one character with nothing much to do says to another, "Listen to this," and for no good reason proceeds to read out the list of names printed on the masthead of *Time*—about a hundred of them. His hearer is enchanted, and cries, "Oh, read it again!" And he does. The *Guardian* has no masthead, but if it had it could supply some flavourous names, particularly from the foreign staff, to please a Saroyan ear: Cecil Sprigge, Darsie Gillie, Terence Prittie, Victor Zorza, Taya Zinkin. What brings such pentecostal variety of names, and personalities, to the *Guardian*? Certainly not the pay, which is comparable to the *Times's* salaries but below the Fleet Street level of the popular Press. If you ask a *Guardian* man he will say, "The job." That's what brought him and that's what keeps him there.[1] It doesn't always keep him, in all cases: some men want or think they must have more money than the *Guardian* pays, or their wives won't live in Manchester, or they succumb to what seems a bigger or better offer. Fleet Street is seeded with journalists who got their early training on the *Guardian*. There is seldom hard feeling over these departures, on either side; but the old hands on the paper will tell you that when men leave, for however good a reason, "something goes out of them".

Why should it? Is there some virtue in the *Guardian* all other papers lack? Who do these *Guardian* men think they are, and what do they think they're doing? Robert Hutchins, when he was Chancellor of the University of Chicago, once said that it was not a very good university but the best there was. *Guardian* men would never put it quite like that, but perhaps that would be a roughly fair statement of how they feel. All papers are more or less unique, but not all papers have a really respectable personality. The *Times*, for one surprising example, is looked down on by the *Guardian*. Not just because the *Times* once fell into the hands of white-slavers and was sold into Northcliffe's harem—that was an unfortunate accident; though it could never have happened to the *Guardian*!—but because they think the *Times* is pompous, hypocritical and censorious. Whatever the *Guardian* does or does not say in public, it cannot abide the personality of the *Times*.[2] If it were possible to imagine such a thing, it might almost be said that the *Times* brings out the beast in the *Guardian*.

For the *Guardian* believes fiercely that its own respectability is real, while the *Times's* is pseudo. The *Times* is often timid, snobbish or orthodox because it is afraid of being wrong; the *Guardian*, which never hesitates on moral issues—and it regards

[1] To supplement their pay, *Guardian* men are allowed to take on extra work—for the weeklies, the B.B.C., etc.

[2] The *Mirror*, which also privately hates and openly despises the *Times*, has called it "a newspaper read by Civil Servants, parsons, the landed gentry and some reactionary schoolteachers".

all real issues as moral—is not afraid of being right. Is it always right? Not even the *Guardian* men would claim that; but they would say that it has the right attitude: it uses its head and its conscience, and always speaks its mind regardless of anything or any person. Of course the *Times*, being frightfully well connected, and carrying as much weight as it does with the interlocking best people, has to be most careful and cannot always be as independent and outspoken as it might like to be—political considerations, you know; wheels within wheels. The *Guardian's* view of this attitude is one of more or less pitying contempt and no quarter. A newspaper should try to influence politics, yes—and every paper that is worth its salt does try—but it must not itself become a political instrument. Once it allows itself to be used as one it has in effect sold its birthright. The *Guardian* has never done that and is determined that it never will.

The men who work for the *Guardian* are proud of the paper, and express their pride in words like this:

"Almost alone among British newspapers it succeeds in avoiding on the one hand the malice and sensationalism of the vulgar press and on the other hand the dreariness and unction of the solemn press."

"Because of its traditions and because it is not content to rest on them."

"It is genuinely independent."

"It's a good paper that is getting better."

"No one works for a paper like the *Guardian* unless he is proud to belong to it (or perhaps very rich) . . . if you read for pleasure not professional purposes, it's the best bet by a long chalk."

"Because it keeps up standards of journalism in Britain which are hard to find in any other newspaper."

"It is the best Liberal daily newspaper in the world."

"It's the newspaper equivalent of a crack regiment."

"Because of its integrity, outspokenness and its own peculiar brand of humour."

"It's honest without being pompous, and liberal without being narrow-minded."

"At critical moments, it talks in plain terms, is not rhetorical or puffed up, but gives pithy form to the arguments current in the most alert and conscientious levels of society."

"It can be and usually is patchy, but it nearly always looks like a paper written by people who enjoy what they are doing for people who enjoy coming upon unexpected good things tucked away in odd places."

"It's a grown-up newspaper written by adults for adults."

In short, the Guardian's men admire and like the paper's personality, and are mainly concerned to preserve it.

The Royal Commission on the Press recognised this phenomenon, observable only in a small section of the quality press: "There are newspapers whose *raison d'être* is neither commercial, political, nor personal, but merely to be themselves, to maintain a certain tradition and to preserve a particular character. The *Times*, the *Manchester Guardian*, and the *Observer* are among them; and the fact that two[1] of these are owned by trusts, while a third enjoys similar safeguards, illumines the character not only of the papers but also of these forms of ownership: they are forms peculiarly suited to famous and long-established papers which have become rather a national institution than a commercial property."

Though the *Guardian* might not like to be thus bracketed with the *Times* it would agree that both papers are national institutions. The distinction the *Guardian* would make between them is that the *Times* is the servant of the Establishment whereas the *Guardian* serves the national conscience. The Establishment has been at times—and may be again—corrupt; but the national conscience is essentially incorruptible. The *Guardian's* role is to admonish and instruct that conscience. Is this beginning to sound dangerously close to spiritual pride, or to that same tendency to pompousness the *Guardian* so despises in the *Times*?

[1] The *Guardian* and the *Observer*.

Does the *Guardian* really think of itself as a minor prophet? Well, not actually; but perhaps it's sometimes a closer thing than the *Guardian* would like to admit. "Upon this earth there can be no much greater responsibility than that involved in the control of a great newspaper. All a man's days and all his powers, all the conscience that is in him, and all the application he can give are surely not too much fittingly to discharge so great a task." C. P. Scott speaking: but for "newspaper" read "kingdom" and it might be any absolute monarch or high priest under the mad misapprehension that his voice, if he really clears his throat, echoes the voice of God. Certainly it's a precarious path, this business of being righteous (even though readable), and the righteous person is in constant danger of missing his footing on the knife-edge; only a vigilant, humorous, almost instinctive sense of balance can save him.

And we must not forget the "something else" in the *Guardian*: "If you read for pleasure, it's the best by a long chalk." A large part of the paper, and the best writing in it, aims to entertain as well as inform. The *Guardian* is full of oddments and little prize packages tucked away here and there. Don't forget, particularly, Alistair Cooke.

Tolerant or addicted readers are likely to overlook lapses into righteousness for the sake of this readability. Not always, of course; not all of them: *Guardian* readers are a mixed lot. Some get furious with it, they write stinging letters to the editor, they cancel their subscriptions, they will no longer have it in the house. On some suddenly posed questions of national conscience—a recent one was the aborted Anglo-French adventure in Suez—a sizeable minority of the *Guardian's* readers violently disagree with the paper's moral stand. They do not deny its right to take a stand: on the contrary, they would think it very wishy-washy if it didn't, but they also assert their own right to differ with it when it is being pig-headed, starry-eyed, self-righteous or just plain stupid. A large section of *Guardian* readers seems to set great store by this mutual independence. An even larger number, of course, like the *Guardian* because it speaks their minds for them. But by and large its readers form an attentively critical audience rather than a reverent one, and the paper can never count on getting unanimous approval or applause. For its part, the *Guardian* accepts the conjectural fact, and rather likes it, that its readers are probably more various in station and opinion than those of most papers.

The *Guardian's* reputation for speaking its mind, after closeting itself with its conscience and the facts of the case, has spread far beyond the circle of its 840,000 readers. Though its circulation is so small, there must be literally millions who know of it by hearsay—vague and thin, but favourable as far as it goes. The same thing is true of other great papers, like *La Prensa* of Buenos Aires: rumour spreads their fame and people who have never seen a copy of the paper in their lives, and would be unable to translate it if they did, pass the rumour along. In this misty sense a paper's influence can thus carry much further than its actual circulation. How else can such outbursts of acclaim as greeted the *Guardian's* centenary be explained? The plaudits came not only, or even most notably, from the paper's readers and supporters but from foreigners, domestic opponents and non-readers, from people to whom the paper had become a household word but who in some cases could not and in some cases would not have a copy in the house. It was the *Guardian's* reputation they were honouring, not its policy—its personality rather than its performance.

In somewhat the same way, the official opinion of the *Guardian* held by the rest of the Press must be distinguished from the unofficial (or actual) opinion. Officially every newspaper is coldly aware or coldly unaware of every other; due to interlinking ownership there are some curious alliances of elephant and mouse, of scorpion and goat, some odd bed-fellows; but there is no love lost between any of them. Birthdays and funerals are exceptional but still official occasions: then they all get as flowery as diplomats. Then they remember that they are all in it together, and speak so kindly of the birthday boy or the dear departed that nobody can possibly believe them. The *Guardian* is old enough to have had its share of these floral tributes, and if it died would certainly get masses of undertaker's garlands.

What do its fellow-newspapers really feel about the *Guardian*? Newspapers don't wear their hearts on their sleeves; in fact, it may be doubted (their personalities being of necessity egocentric beyond the egocentricity of human beings) whether they have a heart, in this sense, at all. Nevertheless, these newspaper personalities are aware of one another and may even be said to have their likes and dislikes, their attractions and antipathies. Among the members of the quality Press, cool customers all, the relation is like that between acquaintances in a club.

The *Times*, as president of the club, has a kind word, a smile and shake of the hand for everybody, including the *Guardian*—who, moreover, as one of the oldest and most distinguished members, rates a slightly firmer shake and more winning smile. The *Daily Telegraph*, a rather grumpy character and a dyed-in-the-wool Tory, confines its greeting to a brusque nod, whenever possible ignoring the *Guardian* altogether. The *Sunday Times*, usually to be seen lunching with the *Daily Telegraph* or agreeing in fierce low tones in a corner of the smoking-room, is of the same exclusive mind. The *Observer*, on the other hand, hails the *Guardian* like an old chum and carries it off to the bar for a drink. And the *News Chronicle*, not a member of the club but a frequent guest, is delighted to be seen in the *Guardian's* company, where it beams with respect.

In the noisy streets outside, where papers are really being peddled, it is like another world entirely. The popular Press are too preoccupied by the flares and bawlings of their savagely competitive street-booths, and by the unceasing effort to lure the crowd away from the other fellow's, to have time for much else. Now and then, however, in a comparative lull, one of them will heave a cobblestone through the club windows or yell a contemptuous epithet at some member who has briefly exposed himself as a target. The *Daily Mirror*, the loudest-mouthed of the lot (and the one that knows how to draw the biggest laugh from the crowd), makes no bones about which member of this toff's society it most dislikes and despises: its pet hate is the *Times*. But, odd as it might seem, there is one member of the quality the *Mirror* not only likes but will stand up for. Of all the papers in Britain, the one that likes the *Guardian* best is probably the *Daily Mirror*.

Who Owns the Guardian?

"Public office is a public trust," said Grover Cleveland, 22nd President of the United States. He had in mind the kind of public office to which a man is either elected or appointed; in C. P. Scott's view, public office could also be assumed. A newspaper that took its responsibilities seriously must consider itself such a public trust. Scott so regarded the *Manchester Guardian*, and saw no discrepancy between this view and the fact that he owned the *Guardian* outright. Private property, if it belonged to a Scott, could be a public trust. He had complete faith in his own integrity and in his sons'; the problem therefore, as it seemed to him, was simply how to ensure the continuance of that wholly trustworthy dynasty.

His action in 1913 of dividing the controlling shares of the paper equally between himself, his two sons and his son-in-law C. E. Montague, was directed to that end. When Montague retired in 1925 he surrendered his quarter share, in accordance with the original agreement. When C. P. Scott died in 1932, his sons Edward and John each became half-owners. Both thought that this arrangement was unsatisfactory and that control of the paper should be more widely shared. No agreement had been reached, however, at the time of Edward's death the following year, leaving John Scott the sole owner.

The *Guardian* at that time was running at a loss, while the *Manchester Evening News* was making sufficient profit to carry both papers. It was the heartless contention of the Inland Revenue, in valuing Edward Scott's half-share for death duties, that the profitless *Guardian* might well cease publication and the profitable *Evening News* be put up for sale on the London newspaper market, where it would undoubtedly fetch a good price.

At this point John Scott called in the lawyers. The eventual result, in 1936, was the Scott Trust.

By the terms of this trust, John Scott surrendered his right to take any profit from the papers ("divested himself of all beneficial interest") and assigned all the shares of both papers to a trust. Dividends were to be paid to the trust and used for the improvement of the newspapers. Since such an agreement could not be made perpetual, the six trustees were empowered to renew the trust from time to time. John Scott, as Chairman of the company, had the power to appoint and dismiss trustees, but no control over the editorial policy or business management of either paper. In his other role, as Managing Director of the *Guardian*, he did control its business side. But the Editor was completely independent of him in all editorial matters and, both by law and custom, remains so.

Two of the six trustees have usually been distinguished public figures unconnected with the *Guardian*; the other four are generally chosen from the paper's management, and always include the *Guardian's* Editor and Managing Director. For a brief period (1940-1946) an American trustee was added: Paul Patterson, publisher of the *Baltimore Sun*. This was to ensure the *Guardian's* survival, or its resurrection. For years before the war the *Guardian*, alone among British daily newspapers, had been barred from Germany—a fact which led the paper's trustees to suppose that if the threatened German invasion succeeded they would be on Hitler's black list and the *Guardian* would be suppressed. A friendly concordat had existed for years between the *Guardian* and the *Baltimore Sun*, and Paul Patterson was therefore asked to become a temporary trustee and to take the deed of trust into his safekeeping while the war lasted. In July 1946 he brought it back to the *Guardian* office in Manchester, where it is now.

It remains a moot point, fiercely argued by the upholders and attackers of "free enterprise", whether ownership of an important paper by one individual or one family is altogether in the public interest; whether such ownership makes for independence of policy or for a biased policy. The evidence is conflicting: in Britain the conduct of the *Manchester Guardian*, which was owned by one family and sometimes by one man until the Scott Trust took it over, shows that a privately-owned paper can earn a reputation for complete integrity. On the other hand, the *Times*, also privately owned, has never succeeded in convincing the public that its policy is independent of its owners and their political connections. The same sort of thing may be seen in the United States, where the New York *Times*, owned first by Adolph Ochs and now by Arthur Sulzberger, has nevertheless established itself as a completely independent newspaper; while the Chicago *Tribune* was always subservient to its master, Colonel McCormick.

As long as our political system permits the private ownership of public utilities, we shall have a continued risk that newspapers may be used for private ends. If a newspaper assumes or attains the position of being a public trust, it would probably be better if it ceased to be a private property. As a matter of principle, it should never be the personal instrument of one man, no matter how convinced he may be of his own integrity. All men who want power are convinced of their integrity.

PART IV

OUR DAILY PILL

I

ONCE, AFTER WRITING a leader, I was summoned by the editor-in-chief, who told me why it wouldn't do. "The way to write a leader," he said, "is to follow the advice of the old Negro preacher: 'First you tell 'em what you're goin' to tell 'em. Then you tell 'em. Then you tell 'em what you've told 'em. Then you sit down.' " Before I sit down, let me tell you what I've told you.

The Press is not our daily bread but our daily sugar pill. If that's true, as I believe it is, then both the *Daily Mirror* and the *Manchester Guardian* come out of the same homeopathic doctor's bag, though they are made up differently to suit different tastes. This is not the accepted view, I know, about the Press in general or these two papers in particular. And yet I suppose a good many people might allow that there's some truth in it if you're talking about a popular tabloid like the *Mirror*, but little if any in the case of a highbrow paper like the *Guardian*. What, in fact, have these two got in common? They have a great deal more in common than is generally supposed.

Each, in its peculiar way, makes just the same claims that are made by all newspapers: that it gives a true report of what's going on in the world, that it has been given a charter to admonish and inform the public, that it speaks for the nation, that it is democracy's daily bread, that it is a responsible institution and, in its way, an instrument of government, that it is an educative force, that it is a reflection of the national state of culture. Neither paper claims very loudly that it supplies daily entertainment—but both do. I prefer the *Guardian* because, as I've said, I like the taste of that particular pill. I also think there are things to be said for, and against, each of these two newspapers.

What good things can we say about the *Mirror*? Quite a few. First, it means well. You don't say! Does Cecil King mean well? Does Hugh Cudlipp mean well? Yes, I think they do. King and Cudlipp are not "good" in C. P. Scott's sense—they don't go in for righteousness—but as journalists they uphold a kind of vulgar decency. Anyhow, I'm not talking about King and Cudlipp but about the *Mirror*, which as a personality transcends both King's and Cudlipp's. The *Mirror's* personality means well—and *Mirror* readers know that, if you don't. "Its manners may not be patrician, but its matter has often proved sound. It has blurted out bluntly truths that needed to be proclaimed which others feared to publish, and conducted useful campaigns in terms the most obtuse could understand. According to its own lights, it has tried to serve the community to the best of its ability."

Doesn't every newspaper *mean* well? Perhaps, but not so obviously: the *Daily Sketch*, for example, or even the *Express*, has a much less well-meaning personality. There are people in Britain—not all of them Oxford dons or Anglican clergy—who seriously believe that the *Mirror* means ill, and has cynically set about corrupting manners and morals because this devil's work is a paying proposition. But these ladies and gentlemen don't read the *Mirror*. If they did, they might continue to dislike and condemn it, but it would have to be on other grounds: they would be forced to admit that in fact the *Mirror* at least means well. The notion that deliberately wicked men run a newspaper for deliberately wicked ends, or "just to make money", is a naïve notion and will not bear examination. It is usually held by people who do not read the paper in question, know no journalists and have never seen the inside of a newspaper office.

Another point that can be cited in the *Mirror's* favour is its immense popularity. This is a democratic reason. In a democracy popularity is synonymous with success. A politician can't be effective unless he is elected, and he can't be elected unless he is popular. A quarter of Britain's population read the

Mirror; they wouldn't read it if they didn't like it. That fact must be chalked up to the *Mirror's* credit, whether or not you put it down as a black mark against Britain.

The *Mirror* uses its popularity to good purpose—on occasion, at least, and according to its lights. "The *Daily Mirror* is much more than just a popular newspaper playing to a vast audience on a basis of sensation and sex appeal. It has a conscience. Frequently its political pages outdo in clarity and depth of thought anything which appears in its more pompous rivals." Thus Mr. Woodrow Wyatt, then (March 1955) a Member of Parliament—Labour, naturally. Yes, the *Mirror* has a conscience, though it might be called mainly a class conscience. It is quick to resent and denounce any outrage, injustice or even slur against the common men and women of Britain. It is notably very much slower to resent outrages, injustices and slurs perpetrated by members of the working class. The *Mirror's* conscience is partial and partisan, that is true; but until the *Mirror* became his champion the common man in Britain had no powerful newspaper he could count on to support and express his views.

The *Mirror* provides daily entertainment for a vast audience, and that can be put to its credit. And the most entertaining part of the act is not the features or the strip cartoons it publishes, but the *Mirror* itself: a super-Cockney (much better value, that, than a Superman) matching his wits and brassy pluck against all comers—and doing very nicely. The *Mirror's* humour is broad and impudent, and sometimes makes its readers grin with delight, as when it announced a competition with the prize of a holiday for two in Jamaica (while Sir Anthony Eden was trying to recuperate there).

The *Mirror* explains political and social problems, when it cares to, in terms so plain that anyone can understand them. Most of the time it takes the realistic view that its readers don't want to be bothered about such things unless they're going to be directly affected by them. When the *Mirror* does print serious news on serious subjects (which it does to a much greater extent than is realised by those who criticise the *Mirror* but don't read it), it tries hard to get the facts right. Its political reporting is biased by the paper's point of view, but that bias and point of view are quite evident and frequently declared. The *Mirror* knows that journalism must simplify in order to interpret.

The *Mirror* speaks out, and it can rise to the occasion. It had strongly opposed Eden's Suez adventure, but at the news that British and French troops were to be withdrawn from Egypt, instead of jeering or saying "I told you so!" the Mirror said to its readers: "Don't just call it a Tory mess. We are all in it. NOW LET US CLOSE THE RANKS", and proceeded to sum up the grim situation and put down some sound suggestions on what to do next.

The *Mirror* encourages humane sentiments in its readers: it is pro-dog and anti-hanging. It is also very pro-baby. On religion it's a little hazy, like most people. It jumps on the Archbishop of Canterbury whenever it gets a chance (as Primate of the Established Church, he's fair game) and laughs its head off at the Red Dean of Canterbury. But it wouldn't dream of jeering at religion: too many of its readers go to church or at least have a soft spot in their hearts for God.

The *Mirror* advertises a hopeful view of the world. I put this on the credit side—it's just a matter of bookkeeping—because the vast majority of newspaper readers also want to believe that the world is improving. Illiterate peasants, of course, know better.

The people who produce the *Mirror*, like the people who read it, believe in its fundamental goodwill and decency. It would be impossible to meet and talk to the men and women who work on the *Mirror* and still hold that they are deliberate corrupters of youth or conscious levellers of public manners and morals. On the contrary, those of them who don't consider that they are providing harmless entertainment (surely not a bad thing in itself) take their roles as interpreters of events and instructors of the public with great seriousness and earnestness, though they may talk deprecatingly and lightly of what they are doing. The men who run the *Mirror* and the staff who produce it believe in democracy in a more-than-British, an almost American way: they believe that the people can always be trusted to do the right thing without being given a lead by their "betters". They don't hold with "betters". And they further believe that the *Mirror* is the principal champion in Britain of this all-out democracy.

The *Mirror* is truly named: it is, whether you like it or not, a mirror of our day.

So much at least can be said to the *Mirror's* credit. Now for some of the black marks. First and most striking of all: it's ugly. I doubt if it knows; I feel certain it doesn't care. For in our civilisation ugliness has not only ceased to matter but is actively furthered under the excuse of "efficiency". The *Mirror's* hideous typography and nasty-looking lay-outs were deliberately designed to attract attention, and that is their whole purpose. Beauty be damned, says the *Mirror*; I want to be looked at. And it works that way. Nevertheless, though in the midst of drab towns and ruined countryside we have almost forgotten why, ugliness is bad; and the *Mirror* is ugly.

The *Mirror* is unscrupulous. It manufactures "news"—but all papers do that—and much of its pseudo-news debases the standard of manners and invades the privacy of defenceless individuals. It usually has some sort of report or rumour to go on, and rarely invents news out of whole cloth; but once it reported in some detail a barbecue given at Balmoral by Princess Margaret which never took place at all.

The *Mirror* is vulgar. It might not argue this point directly, but would object to the word "vulgar" as snobbish and upper-class. Why not say "it has the common touch"? All right; that's saying the same thing in genteel euphemism, i.e., vulgarly.

The *Mirror* is sensational. It accepts the charge and glories in it. For papers that do not sensationalise news, the *Mirror* has nothing but scorn. If a newspaper doesn't make itself attractive to readers by sensational treatment of the news and by sensational make-up, why should anybody read it? The *Mirror* holds that only a few fuddy-duddies, pompous asses and the so-called intelligentsia read the non-sensational Press: Let them; everyone else reads the *Mirror*, or should and will.

The *Mirror* over-simplifies. This charge is often brought against journalism in general, but it has special relevance to the *Mirror*. By the news it chooses to report and by the way it reports that news, the *Mirror* foists on its readers over-simplified, parochial and therefore false notions about the world. The *Mirror* is notoriously sentimental and not ashamed of it: it's not only sentimental about dogs, which is bad enough, but about human beings, which is worse. Over-simplification falsifies by leaving out facts; sentimentality falsifies by adding fiction. The *Mirror* might retort that its world is no smaller, no more parochial and no more fictitious than those of other popular papers on both sides of the Atlantic. It might even say that it's the best of a bad lot—except that the *Mirror* couldn't admit that the popular Press is bad.

To many people in Britain the *Mirror's* personality is hateful. During the newspaper strike which shut down all London newspapers for 26 days in the spring in 1955, a speaker on a B.B.C. programme said: "Anything which will stop the circulation of the *Daily Mirror* or the *News of the World* is a first-class thing." Earlier the same year, in a debate in the House of Commons, the *Mirror* was indirectly attacked as a deliberate corrupter of public morals: "The *Week-end Mail* and *Reveille*[1] are classic examples. There is no question that they tend to corrupt morals, and are published for that purpose." Neither of these statements was true, but the hatred behind them was obviously genuine.

Though quite probably it doesn't mean to, and doesn't think of itself as doing any such thing, the *Mirror* helps to lower the moral and intellectual standards of the country. This searching criticism of the *Mirror* appeared in an unlikely place: the Preface to the 1956 edition of *Crockford's Clerical Directory*: "The Press is both a symptom and an encouragement of the decline

[1] Published by the *Daily Mirror*.

in absolute values so manifest in the life of the country today. . . . There is not so great a gulf as might be supposed between the *Daily Mirror* and the present deplorable condition of English metaphysics and moral philosophy." But this charge would hardly be taken seriously by the *Mirror*. Metaphysics! Moral philosophy! says the *Mirror* with a great guffaw, what have they got to do with anything that matters?

At first sight, it might seem a little far-fetched to blame the *Mirror* for the sad state of metaphysics and moral philosophy—rather like blaming Al Capone for the lawlessness that was encouraged in the United States by Prohibition. Yet it cannot be denied that Al Capone did his bit to further that lawlessness because it suited his book. So does "the decline in absolute values", with the consequent confusion in manners and morals, suit the *Mirror's* book. The *Mirror* is quite confident that its sister publication, the *Sunday Pictorial*, will soon outstrip that old mastodon, *News of the World*, and for one simple reason: *News of the World*, though it is extremely sex-conscious, still clings to the outmoded, moralistic view of sex as something delightfully furtive and shocking: while the *Pictorial* (like the *Mirror*—and the rising generation) takes sex at its declined but up-to-date value, as just a bit of good healthy fun. Everybody feels that way now, says the *Mirror*, and the way everybody feels is the right way to feel.

The *Mirror* has much the same mentality and moral outlook as a Butlin camp. In pre-Butlin days the line between the eccentric and the individual was never effectively drawn in England. But from the mass point of view the individual *is* eccentric. And if the *Mirror* succeeds in ignoring "metaphysics and moral philosophy" out of existence, the individual will vanish: he will either have to conform voluntarily or be put in an institution—perhaps a state-run Butlin camp.

2

What a pleasure it is to praise the *Guardian*—and so easy, too. It is civilised, kindly, tolerant and humane. It entertains and instructs (or shouldn't we say "instructs and entertains"?—no, let's leave it that way) a small but educated audience. While the *Guardian* is in good-humoured and mannerly charge of the meeting, we can be sure that no catcalls, stink-bombs or heckling will interrupt. It explains, it elucidates, it expatiates on political and social problems in terms so reasonable and persuasive that it leaves most of us feeling (mostly) that the thing couldn't have been better put.

But the *Guardian* doesn't mind being unpopular. Sometimes it enrages quite a lot of its readers. Just after the Queen's Coronation, the *Guardian* printed a cartoon of Low's captioned *Morning After*, and showing a TV set and a bleary Britannia overlooking the rubbishy aftermath of a "£100,000,000 spree", a litter of toys, doll-duchesses, a broken drum. This comment was not taken well by a great many people, who did not regard it as either reasonable or persuasive, and said so with some heat. The *Guardian* took the dead cats and the cancelled subscriptions in good part and went on speaking its mind. Admitting that the cartoon had been "a cold douche", and perhaps a little too close to the event, a *Guardian* leader (in A. P. Wadsworth's unmistakable tones) said: "The meaning of Low's cartoon, it seems to us, was that now we have done honour to the Queen, cemented the bonds of Commonwealth, and had our jollification, we should remember that we live in a world of cruel reality. . . . Many of us—but hardly all—have had a deep spiritual experience. Now we have to settle down. . . ."

The *Guardian* too encourages humane sentiments. But it reads rather more into "humane" than the *Mirror* does. The *Guardian*, like the *Mirror*, is pro-dog and anti-hanging; and it once ran a series of articles exposing the cruelties of the traffic in Irish horses, shipped to slaughter-houses in England and on the Continent. But its humanity extends to foreign nations and alien ideas; it accepts Communists, Arabs, Nasser and John Foster Dulles as human beings, for whom there is often something to be said—and whenever there is, the *Guardian* says it. This naturally infuriates those who take the orthodox

Russian or the orthodox American view of the world as being composed of our side (good) and their side (bad). It also brings the *Guardian* under suspicion of being an idealist, and unrealistic.

The 170,000 *Guardian* buyers don't consider it unrealistic, at bottom. Quite the contrary. The *Guardian's* view of the world, which it refrains from advertising but which is there to be seen just the same, is cautiously sceptical, kindly but disillusioned. There is no sentimentality here about industrial production and civilised progress going hand in hand, nor loose talk about melodramatic "solutions" or melodramatic defeats. If the world has perceptibly wobbled to the left in the 136 years the *Guardian* has been watching it, there have been equally perceptible wobbles to the right. The *Guardian* takes a reasonably hopeful view of the future, but it remembers enough about the past to keep its hopes under control. The men who make up the *Guardian* today would give two cheers (not three) for democracy and two (not three) for the *Guardian* itself, as one of the quieter advocates of a democracy that is only partly civilised.

And how pleasant to be able to say, "without fear of contradiction", that the *Guardian* is one of the ornaments of the Press. It is not one of those unexceptionably high-minded papers that put you to sleep by their droning delivery, or detract from what they say by always saying it badly. The *Guardian* is one of those rare newspapers where good writing and good journalism meet. It has been said that what journalism needs is more poets, but the *Guardian* has shown that prose-writers will do. The *Guardian* is a good newspaper, well written. What more could a newspaper reader ask?

The *Guardian*, like the *Mirror*, is truly named: it is a guardian not only of British liberties and the democratic process but, above all, of civilised values.

And now for the other side of the coin. What can be said in the *Guardian's* disfavour? First, it is ineffectual. It is a paper with a circulation of only 170,000 in a nation of 51 million. The *Guardian* is supported by no party and no class. Its readers are not an effective group, politically or socially. Now that the Liberal Party is moribund the *Guardian* has become a political ghost—liberal with a small "l".

The *Guardian* is a somewhat patchy paper, as the men who work on it admit. It's good, but not good all the way through, not every day nor in every department. And this patchiness applies not only to the news it reports (or fails to report) but to the quality of the writing. Sometimes the writing is no better than average, sometimes it's dull, sometimes turgid. The poorest writing is likely to be found in its anonymous reporters' despatches and in its special articles by experts. It's an unevenly edited, unevenly written paper.

Lightness of touch doesn't necessarily argue lightness of mind—often quite the contrary. But now and then an unbecoming and rather artificial levity creeps into the *Guardian's* normal tone of voice, and this strikes an uncomfortably false note, like an affected accent or a professor being kittenish. At other times the *Guardian* can be over-didactic. There is a cant of the intelligentsia, a higher and more disingenuous variety than the sentimentality of the *Mirror*, and the *Guardian* is not wholly free from it. Personally I prefer disingenuous cant to the ingenuous kind—if only because there's more hope of clearing the mind than the heart.

The odd idea that the *Guardian* is light-minded, or more so than is generally supposed, was put into my head by some of the *Guardian* staff themselves. For their part they thought it odd that anyone should find a great contrast between the *Guardian* and the *Mirror*. As one of them put it, the *Mirror* and the *Guardian* are opposite sides of the same coin. With obvious differences in accent and tone, both have the same humanist, ex-Liberal point of view. There is more humanity in the *Mirror*, said one of my *Guardian* friends, for the *Mirror* speaks warmly and coarsely to the masses, while the *Guardian* soliloquises for the intelligentsia. But the two papers are much more alike than they are different, and they recognise their kinship. The *Mirror* is freer to speak a kind word for the *Guardian* than vice versa, for the *Guardian* has a social reputation to keep up, and a lot of its readers would be shocked to learn that it doesn't think the *Mirror* is so bad, really.

Their non-religious faith brings the two papers closest together: they are both pro-Man and neutral against Heaven. The *Mirror* aims primarily to entertain but also tries to instruct —according to its limited imagination and paltry ambitions. The *Guardian* aims primarily to instruct, but is delighted when it is found entertaining. The *Mirror*, pretending to be a hearty, earthy lover of life, in fact is a shrewd money-grubber and power-grabber. To escape facing the facts of existence, so as not to be forced to contemplate the true human condition, the *Mirror* must continually struggle to expand, to "get things done". The *Guardian*, pretending to be an elderly and disinterested bystander, a kind of Greek chorus commenting with pity on the inexorable action of the play, in fact is delighted when its influence seems in any way effective. To escape from its suspicion that nothing can be done, so as not to be forced to contemplate the horror of a world out of man's control, the *Guardian* must continually diversify, change the subject, "distribute the risk".

On balance, I prefer the *Guardian* to the *Mirror*. For one thing, I think the *Guardian* might really be more useful in the long run —if the run is long: perhaps the only possible kind of spoke-in-the-wheel to the Juggernaut of Progress, which seems bound to crush us all but may be impeded. I prefer geological time to Greenwich time. I prefer Thousand-Year Plans, which come to nothing or come to something different from what their planners intended, to Five-Year Plans, which are simply succeeded by other Five-Year Plans, either cancelling or endorsing their predecessor, thus reducing us to the *Mirror*, or ingenuous cant.

The *Guardian* and the *Mirror* are fundamentally alike but outwardly different—far enough apart to represent between them the whole spectrum of journalism. The *Mirror* is not the most extreme example of the sensational Press, but it is the most popular; and though the *Guardian* may not be in every respect the best of the quality Press, it is certainly their worthy representative. Though the *Mirror* is flawed, it is the truest mirror we have of our culture (i.e., our expenditure), as the *Guardian* is one of the truest guardians of our civilisation (i.e., our capital).

3

The main business of the Press, supposedly, is news, as the main business of banks is money. It might surprise the public to discover how incurious many bankers are about the real nature of money and how unclear they are about it. In just the same way, and perhaps to a greater extent, most journalists are incurious about the real nature of news and just as unclear about it. This particular question has been begged for so long that it now seems either self-evident or insoluble. Ask a journalist "What is news?" and you'll get one of a number of answers, ranging from "It's what interests *me*" (meaning "the paper I work on") to "How the hell should I know?" (meaning "I just work here").

Perhaps the neatest as well as the most generally accepted definition of news is "what happened yesterday". I remember once totting up the front-page news stories (the news of the day considered most important) in a good provincial newspaper, in America. Of the eleven stories on the page, seven had not happened at all—in the sense of man biting dog, or even of dog biting man. Some of the speculations about the future, and there were many, might have come true, but so far they were just speculations. If news is what happened yesterday, the newspapers print an awful lot of phoney news.[1] But we have

[1] An amusing example of manufactured news appeared in two recent issues of the New York *Herald Tribune's* Paris edition. On February 6, 1957, the main headline on the front page read:

DULLES BELIEVES ISRAEL, EGYPT
WILL OBEY RESOLUTIONS OF UN

and the following day the main headline was

EISENHOWER BELIEVES
ISRAEL WILL WITHDRAW

For two days the biggest news the paper could find was what an official *said* he thought!

seen how the practical definition of news varies from paper to paper. Journalists have never been very keen on defining news theoretically, except in a parlour-game spirit. An editor whose faith in the news was simple, like C. P. Scott, took news for granted: news was the sacred facts. An equally inexact but more inclusive description might be, "News is what the press produces". It isn't only physics that's getting more complicated; we now know that facts, like the atom, can be split.

I musn't push the analogy with banks too far, but there is one striking similarity between banks and the Press: both to a great extent manufacture their product, though they are not popularly supposed to. By far the greatest part of the world's "money" is issued by banks in the form of credit. Most of the world's "news" is manufactured by the Press itself: interviews with important men, reports on grave situations, press conferences, press investigations, political surveys, "informed speculation", etc., etc.

Most "hard news" falls into the Press's lap like meteorites or manna from heaven: murder and suicide, rape, war, pestilence, famine, catastrophes of all kinds. This bad news is the best news to the Press: it's not only exciting to read but it comes ready-made. Mongers of sensational news, like the *Mirror*, admitting that the supply of this sort of news is unsteady, meet the daily demand for sensation in two ways: by dressing up small news to look big, and by ballyhooing daily features. There is no essential difference between the inevitable screaming front-page headline of the *Mirror* and the "running story" from Reuter's of a diplomatic conference: both are manufactured news. They are said to have happened big; actually, they either didn't happen at all or they only happened a little.

Some of the more exacting followers of C. P. Scott still insist that their paper deals in sacredly regarded facts. That is probably true in spots, although they conveniently overlook the other spots in the paper that are profanely opinionated rather than sacredly factual. A large part of the Press has in effect abandoned the pretence of dealing exclusively with facts, or the pretence that their source is invariably as pure as the Pierian spring. A great many newspapers, for example, make no bones about printing gossip. They still, officially at least, exclude rumour (except from the gossip columns, or unless it can be attributed to a "hitherto unimpeachable source", when it rises from "rumour" to "speculation" or "inside information").

Actually, news includes a great deal of rumour. A journalist friend of mine, on assignment in Central America, once had occasion to hire a "stringer" (a local correspondent) in a small town there. Since there was no newspaper in the town, the most likely candidate was one of the few English-speaking inhabitants who seemed to know his way around. He was duly hired and his duties explained to him. A few days later my friend looked up the new stringer to see how he was getting on. As yet he had found nothing to report but he had prepared himself for any emergency by buying a large notebook which he had divided into two sections; the first was headed "Rumours", the second "False Rumours".

Claud Cockburn, once a prized *Times* correspondent, during the last war put out a brilliant weekly news-sheet that was read by the small number of people who constituted "everybody" in London. His views on the nature of news were also unorthodox:

> I went about saying that rumours were just as important, just as significant, just as—in the last analysis—"valid" as "facts."
>
> This shocked people horribly, although if you pressed them and asked whether it was not true that ninety per cent of "information received" by such serious persons as Ambassadors and Chiefs of Police really consists in significant rumours and rumours which can be interpreted by the person who knows enough rumours, they were usually bound to admit that this is indeed the case. . . . Unless one is God, how on earth can one tell truth from rumour in less than perhaps fifty years? And fifty years is too long to wait if one is in the business of issuing a weekly newspaper.

Cockburn was honest enough—or cynical enough, if you prefer—to include rumour in his definition of news. Few editors would agree with him without drawing a line, but whatever they may say, their practice follows his precept. The only journalists who are consistently successful in keeping rumour and gossip out of the news are the Communists. The Communist Press, an avowed instrument of government, is dedicated to the proposition that facts equal propaganda equals truth. The facts are chosen, the propaganda ordered, and the truth announced. It's much simpler than with us. And the Russians have a great contempt for the confusions of the Western Press, which all stem from this inadmissable *search* for news. "News" in Russia is issued as a valuable, State-controlled ration.

When Ilya Ehrenburg, one of the dark stars of Communist journalism, visited the United States a few years ago, he was much bothered by reporters who pried into what he considered irrelevant personal questions—the one that moved him to most sardonic mirth was whether a suit he was having made at a New York tailor's was to have trousers with a buttoned fly or with a zipper. There, he said triumphantly, you have a picture of the Western Press, which concerns itself with gossip: buttons or zipper, that is all they care to know about. In the doctrinaire Communist view, our Free Press makes too little distinction between public news (which is the Press's only business) and private news (which is none of its business). Moreover, say the Communists, nobody but they know what news is fit to publish, or what news really is.

Our defence to this is apt to be: "The truth shall make you free"—by which we mean that if everybody talks continuously at the top of his lungs, somebody from time to time will probably say something true, somebody else may hear it, and it may have some good effect, by and large. Nevertheless, we have an uneasy suspicion that there should be some distinction between public and private news, and that the Press doesn't make the distinction clear—no doubt because of the general confusion about what news really is. Public or private, the news must affect our individual lives, it must be translatable into our personal terms, before we will pay attention to it. Even the news in Russian papers, which couldn't be more public, can be so translated, I should imagine. Everything *Pravda* or *Izvestia* publishes means some action or threat of action by the Government; the trick is to see: "How is that going to affect *me*?" We read the newspapers that way in time of war, when all governments are grey. In peacetime, public news for most of us is just something to quack about, and it rolls off our backs; the news that really concerns us comes by word of mouth or by mail. The opening door, the doctor's verdict, the expected letter, the telegram that says "death" or "life": this is the kind of news that comes home to us. Perhaps it is the only real news there is.

Nevertheless, we feel that there should be bigger news than this and the Press continually assures us that indeed there is. The Press keeps on telling it, in big headlines; big good news and big bad news. The big good news is mainly manufactured, not so much because the Press is sanguine by nature as that it is committed to the encouraging notion of progress. The big bad news is what has actually happened. When our candidate is elected or the war ends, we may call the news both big and good; but what will it be called by the people who voted for the other man, or who lost the war? No, really good news, in the public sense, is either incredible or beyond our understanding. And yet we crave it, its absence seems wrong, we want it to be. The Press, which is as human as the rest of us, shares this craving and gropes for big good news—however incredible or beyond our understanding. When the New York *Times* printed the text of Einstein's theory it was in this mystical and groping spirit. It's rather like the poem in which Thomas Hardy said that if someone asked him on Christmas Eve to come with him to the stable to see the oxen kneel before the Christ Child, he would go along, "hoping it might be so". The hope was that Einstein had found a large piece of truth—even if nobody, or almost nobody, could understand it; and in that hope the New

York *Times's* editor was willing to bow his uncomprehending head, and take the whole congregation of the *Times* to their knees with him.

In less than two generations science has become untranslatable, and its speculations about the world come to us more and more faintly, like the dwindling shouts of a search-party that have disappeared into an enormous maze. The news they succeed in sending back to us (with the Press as messenger) often seems contradictory of earlier bulletins; the gist of it comes across as a progressive disillusionment with accepted facts and an immense widening and deepening of the unknowable. But this is depressing and therefore unacceptable to our optimistic habit of mind—as if, with all our advantages, we were just catching up with Socrates, and as it were from behind! So the Press continues to hail scientific "discoveries" (the substitution of a new theory for an abandoned one) as if they were real news, big news and good news. And the public, official view of science's search for knowledge is one of untiring hope and faith. In private, however, there is scepticism and doubt, and not just among illiterate peasants either.

The only big news, private and public, that human beings are really concerned about is news of life and death. There has been no new news on either subject for some time—nearly 2,000 years, in fact. The Resurrection was tremendous good news, if true; the best news ever reported. But though it has been told wherever Christian missionaries have gone and a large proportion of the earth's population must have heard it, it is still widely disbelieved or believed only in a poetic or mystical sense, as "an honourable thought"[1] or an incomprehensible symbol. Even those Christians who believe that the Resurrection was an event that actually happened and a demonstration that individual human beings are literally immortal would nowadays hesitate to apply it without

[1] As Emily Dickinson called it:

> . . . *That we've immortal place*
> *Though pyramids decay,*
> *And kingdoms, like the orchard,*
> *Flit russetly away.*

qualification to their own personal lives and deaths. As for agnostics and unbelievers, they have accepted and spread the persistent rumour that the news of the Resurrection was much exaggerated or downright false.

The Press is only a reflection of the world it reports, and like the world it's quite unable to recognise or accept really good news—a saint for the ages, a hero both immediate and lasting, a revelation of permanent truth; it can only exaggerate or minimize, ignore, misreport or doubt, just like the rest of us. Big bad news it can't miss; big good news it never sees—though it pretends a lot of little good news is big, and manufactures all the big good news it can. What keeps the Press going is mainly snippets: some news, much gossip, loads of rumours—not to speak of all the features, extras, special acts and entertaining etceteras.

The biggest piece of clap-trap about the Press is that it deals almost exclusively, or even mainly, with news.

4

And the next-biggest piece of clap-trap is that the Press has enormous power. This delusion is persistent and widespread. It is taken for granted by the public-at-large, who are apt to be impressed by anything that is said three times; it is continually advertised by the Press itself, and it is cherished by Press lords, some of whom, at least, should know better. The Hutchins "Commission on the Freedom of the Press", which represented a more-than-usually-intelligent public-at-large in the United States, not only took the power of the Press at the Press's own valuation but thought it very alarming:

> We have the impression that the American people do not realise what has happened to them. They are not aware that the communications revolution has occurred. They do not appreciate the tremendous power which the new instruments and the new organisation of the Press place in the hands of a few men."[1]

[1] But again the reader should remember that the Hutchins Commission included all communications under "Press"—radio, cinema and television, as well as newspapers.

In what way is the Press supposed to be so powerful? The general notion is that the Press can form, control or at least strongly influence public opinion. Can it really do any of these things? Hugh Cudlipp, Editorial Director of the *Mirror*, and a man who should know something about the effect of newspapers on public opinion, doesn't share this general notion about their power. He thinks newspapers can echo and stimulate a wave of popular feeling, but that's all: "A newspaper may successfully accelerate but never reverse the popular attitude which common-sense has commended to the public." In short, it can jump aboard the bandwagon, once the bandwagon's under way, and exhort others to jump aboard too; but it can't start the bandwagon rolling, or change its direction after it's started.

Like other habit-forming pills, the Press can stimulate or depress, but it cannot cure. It can fan fear and hatred of another nation (when the fear and hatred are there, waiting to be fanned) but it cannot make peace.[1] As more and more people have painful reason to know, the Press has a nasty kind of power—the same kind of power a bully has, of hurting somebody smaller and weaker than himself. An individual's only defence against the Press is the law of libel, but considerable harm and much pain can be caused without going as far as to commit an actionable libel. Journalists themselves generally have a horror of being interviewed, "written up" or even noticed by the Press—they know too well from their own experience how inept and cruel a distortion[2] the result is likely to be.

[1] William Randolph Hearst, in his day the biggest of American Press tycoons, deliberately used his papers to embroil the United States with Spain in 1898. In the process of fomenting war-fever, he sent correspondents to Cuba, then in half-hearted revolt against Spain, to get propaganda photographs and inflammatory stories. When one of them protested that he could find no suitable photographs, Hearst cabled him in a fury: "You furnish the pictures and I'll furnish the war."

[2] Even in photographs—which, in the lying phrase, "cannot lie". They can be made to lie (e.g., to bolster a point of propaganda, as Northcliffe was one of the first to discover. When he was using the *Daily Mail* to try to get Asquith out as Prime Minister and Lloyd George in, he once issued this order: "Get a smiling picture of Lloyd George, and underneath put the caption '*Do It Now*', and get the worst possible picture of Asquith and label it '*Wait and See*'." Since Northcliffe's day this technique has been developed much further.) In spite of the reluctance of picture editors to admit it, the camera can also distort. In the office where I worked there used to be a saying: "The camera distorts. The TV camera distorts absolutely."

Nine times out of ten, as they know, ineptness is to blame rather than conscious cruelty; but there is always that tenth case. And a blundering friendly hand can be as heavy as an unfriendly fist. The Press is often like a clumsy giant who gives you a pat on the back and knocks the wind out of you, if he doesn't cause internal injuries. I remember once coming upon an elderly professor of my university who had just been "written up" by the paper I worked on. When he saw me, tears came into his eyes, and he said, "What have I done to them? What have I done to deserve this?" He was deeply wounded by the article, and regarded it as an extremely unkind caricature. Knowing that it had been written by one of his former students who liked and admired the professor, I tried to reassure him that it was at least kindly meant; I don't think I succeeded.

The Press has a negative power—to titillate, alarm, enrage, amuse, humiliate, annoy, even to drive a person out of his community or his job. But of the positive power to which it pretends, and of which the Press lords dream—to make and break governments, to swing an election, to stop a war or start a revolution—there is no tangible evidence. Its vaunted might is a gigantic spoof. Professor David Mitrany, speaking in 1932 on *The Press and International Relations*, put the case with delicate irony: "There is no need to spend time in an attempt to show how great is the influence of the Press. It is greater in certain fields than in others. It is greater, one could say, in any field in which the knowledge and interest of the man in the street is lesser. For in that case the reading public is apt to think that the Press speaks with the voice of Authority; while the authorities are apt to assume that the Press is speaking with the voice of the People. . . ."

Everyone has heard of the "power of the Press"; no one has seen it. The greatest believers in this exaggerated "power" and the loudest promoters of it are, naturally, the Press lords themselves. One of the most deluded of these, not even excepting Northcliffe or Beaverbrook, was Robert McCormick, publisher of the Chicago *Tribune* (still emblazoned with his modest motto: "The world's greatest newspaper"). McCormick, and of course his paper, were always in bitter opposition to the Roosevelt Democrats, as well as to the liberal element in his own Republican Party. A story used to be told about the Chicago *Tribune*—no doubt apocryphal but in essence true: that one of the janitors in the *Tribune* building always bet against any political candidate the paper supported, and gave odds to boot; and that he found this side-line so profitable that he was able to buy two sizeable blocks of flats. The men in the street are better able than the Press lords to judge the "power" of the Press: in spite of all the kow-towing and brass bands, they can see that the Emperor has no clothes on.[1]

The people in Chicago who bought the *Tribune* didn't buy it to find out how to cast their votes: they bought it in spite of its advice and its bias, because on the whole they liked its personality and found it entertaining. Does this seem to argue a too shrewd, calm and sensible attitude on the part of the ordinary newspaper reader? The Press is generally appreciated by the public for what it is rather than for what it pretends to be: they don't feel it as a power in their lives but as a perquisite in their working day.

5

Unlike the ordinary newspaper reader, politicians and publicists are more apt to take the Press at its own valuation. Lord Attlee sees the growth of the popular Press as dangerous, not because it is powerful in a political sense, but because it is too light-minded: "You are getting today papers that have no point of view and are only entertainment. The danger is that they prevent people from considering serious matters."

This is surely a more sensible and realistic sizing-up, and a

[1] As noted before, during the 20 years (1932-1952) of Democratic Party government in America under Roosevelt and Truman, something like 85% of the American Press was owned or controlled by Republicans: the majority of American newspaper readers were being continually exhorted to vote Republican but continued to vote Democrat.

more really damaging criticism of the popular Press's performance, than the usual diatribes against the menace of a powerful and sinister yellow Press. As long ago as 1930 a critic of the Press was saying: "One doubts . . . if the British public's faith in its newspapers can very much longer survive; so amazingly blatant are the methods with which the newspaper-owners, in these days of acute competition, hope to attract readers, so impertinent are the claims of these owners to a right to control the political destinies of our country. Surely it cannot be long before the masses awake to the fact that has been in possession of well-informed people for some time past: that our Press is guilty (*a*) of forging weapons that give it power to exert excessive and illegitimate influence on the national destinies, and (*b*) of vulgarising the mind of the nation."

So far the masses have given no signs of "awaking" in any such sense, and the British public's appetite for newspapers has grown by leaps and bounds. In the past 15 years, says Francis Williams:

> the British public have become the most avid readers of newspapers on earth. At least thirty million newspapers—national, provincial, morning and evening—now go into British homes every working day; on Sundays even more . . . last year (1955) 88·3 per cent of the adult population read at least one morning paper on an average day. . . .[1] Within the last two decades total newspaper circulations have increased at a rate nearly ten times that of the growth in population. . . . The serious journals of information and opinion, the *Times*, the *Manchester Guardian* and, on a slightly more 'popular' level the *Daily Telegraph*, although they still account for only nine per cent of total newspaper sales have risen in circulation at a rate even higher than the general one. . . . Despite a common myth to the contrary, not only is it true to say that the public for intelligent serious journalism

[1] The U.S. is far behind, per capita. Total newspaper sales there in 1956 were 57 million daily (an increase of 1 million over 1955)—about one newspaper for every three people. Sunday papers sold 47 million.

has expanded remarkably since before the war but it is now a far higher portion of the whole than it has ever been.

Nevertheless the most significant feature of this revolution lies elsewhere. It is to be found in the opening-up of an entirely new market, the spread of the habit of newspaper reading to millions of the mass public who formerly rarely read a newspaper and still more rarely bought one. . . . More than 90 per cent of this new market has been captured by two newspapers, the *Daily Mirror* and the *Daily Express*, and some 57 per cent of it by the *Mirror* alone. . . . The more serious of the popular papers have not only failed to capture any of the new reading public but are losing ground steadily to those with a formula more attractive to a mass readership. . . . The *Mirror* has won its success by ignoring nearly all traditional standards of news value, and by developing the magazine feature side of journalism to an extent never previously seen in daily journalism . . .

The same observer, commenting on the dwindling number of provincial papers, says: "We are moving more and more towards a pattern of journalistic uniformity that cannot help, I think, but have a damaging effect upon the vigour and variety of a good deal of national life." And he noted that the *Daily Sketch*, certainly the most vulgar daily tabloid now published in Britain, in the first six months of 1956 had "dredged from its journeys into the depths nearly as many new readers as the total *Guardian* circulation".

6

In a society that encourages competition, it is always theoretically possible that one competitor may swallow up the others. In the British Press at present the obvious competition is fiercest between papers of the same group, popular *v.* popular, quality *v.* quality. The competition is for survival, and in the struggle weaker papers have been and will continue to be swallowed up—or in some cases killed but not eaten. But the tigers are fighting other tigers, and leave the field-mice to their own small wars: the popular Press and the quality Press seem to co-exist in peace, or at least in mutual forbearance. I suggest that this co-existence is largely an illusion and may be merely temporary, and that the forbearance (which is all on the side of the popular Press—for how should Switzerland attack Russia?) may not last.

The real competition, in short, although it has not yet broken into open war, is between the popular Press and the quality Press. And the stake in that coming war will be survival. If the present trend continues—that is, if the more successful popular papers continue to capture more and more new readers—then the popular Press will win, and eventually become what it already claims to be: the only Press worth mentioning, the only Press there is. It will first kill off "the more serious of the popular papers" and then turn its attention to the only competition remaining: the papers of the quality Press. Perhaps it may be decided to let them live, as harmless traditional curiosities like the Beefeaters at the Tower; perhaps some of them may be taken over and continued as "prestige advertising" (as Cecil King tried the *London Magazine*); or perhaps they may be "livened up"—streamlined a bit and translated into plain terms for the common man. Such an absorption of the quality by the popular Press would no doubt be quite acceptable to the great majority of newspaper readers.

It would of course not satisfy the minority, those addicts who feel, or who think they feel, that the only paper worth reading is the *Guardian* or the *Times*; but this minority could be dealt with. Time would take care of the elderly. The London *Morning Post* and the Boston (Mass.) *Evening Transcript* were once looked upon as daily necessities by their devotees; they and their readers have disappeared, but London and Boston remain. As for the younger generation, they can generally be persuaded that the modern present, which is theirs, is preferable to the old-fashioned past, which is not. And would they necessarily be wrong? Whatever the Press of the twenty-first century may be like, I see no reason to suppose that it will be a less faithful social historian than the Press has always been. In that role, indeed, the Press cannot fail. Wrong, incomplete or sketchy as it is in detail, its continuous, massive accumulation of facts, fancies, irrelevancies, rumours, gossip and kaleidoscopic gimcracks cannot help reflecting the character, prejudices, tone and habits of its day.

Certain papers regard themselves as "newspapers of record", that is, they have two audiences in mind—their own, and future historians. This is why papers like the *Times* of London, the *Times* of New York, the *Daily Telegraph* and the *Manchester Guardian* often disregard the other demands on their readers' time and print all the details they can get about "that obscure revolution in Bolivia". It is with an eye quite as much, or more, on the future reader that they print the full text of speeches and treaties that most of their present readers, they know, will skip. And such papers do add their dusty piles to the attic where the archives of history are kept. They furnish a diary of their times which is useful and necessary to historians (who do not fail to point out, however, that this record is not always complete, trustworthy or accurate).

The popular Press doesn't give a damn for history. It regards one live reader as worth two unborn ones, and historical archives as stuffy and dead; its own are scrappy and disorganised but bursting with "human interest". Nevertheless, without knowing or caring a rap, the popular Press is recording history all the time—social history, that is. Not parliamentary debates, the pronouncements of big-wigs, and other solemn stuff, but "how it is with the country and the people". It's a dreadful thought, no doubt, but in its embarrassing way the popular Press may come nearer to telling the real record, the human story. It knows instinctively—and what's more, has the courage of its instinct—that people are more important, more interesting, more *news* than events (and certainly than pseudo-events) are. Its way of telling about people is often a brutal, crude or sentimental travesty on what they are really like. But which is the more preposterous caricature of our day—the sketches of this "lightning artist" or the stiffly posed and dressed-up portrait painted by "the papers of record"? Slap-dash style, crass technique, vulgar colours and all, the popular Press does manage to strike off a likeness which the quality Press, in spite of its pains and polish, misses. Well, the social historians of the future will have to judge which of these piles of old newspapers is more useful for their purpose. No doubt both piles will be needed.

And for the present we must include them both. The Press is newspapers, all of them. The Press claims to be the historian of our day; and no one disputes that claim, except the small voice of books. But if the Press claims further that it knows and tells (by exclusive copyright) the story of what is really happening, we simply don't believe it. The Austrian novelist, Robert Musil, has put the case with discerning and devastating candor: "Every schoolboy could understand the details of what was going on, but as regards the whole there was nobody who quite knew what was really happening, except a few persons, and even they were not sure whether they knew." The Press is a net to catch the wind. A net cannot fail to trap what is blown into its meshes, and the Press does catch some birds of passage and some odd tail-feathers, which show which way the wind is blowing, for the moment. But the meshes of the net are wide and many a bird slips through uncaught—perhaps the most valuable birds of all. As for the wind, it remains invisible and and uncatchable; we cannot tell whence it comes nor whither it goes.

If you travelled from Berlin to Paris to London in, say, 1936 (when most of the experts, journalistic and otherwise, were reassuring everybody that there would be no war), it was like going from one walled city to another. The news of what was happening was not in the newspapers—not so you could recognise it, although it was buried there, as it so often is, unperceived by the newspaper's own editors—the news was in the streets, and the people in the streets knew it if the experts and the journalists didn't. The news was that war was coming, and that it was being made in Germany.

The Press doesn't tell what's really happening because it doesn't really know—until afterwards, and then it can never pick up all the pieces.

7

The Press bears almost the same relation to news as the American drugstore to pharmacy: it is possible to get a prescription filled at a drugstore, but drugs are a very small part of its business, and most of its customers are attracted by the soda fountain, the book and magazine racks, the tobacco counter, the fountain pens, rubber goods, etc., etc. There are still a few old firms which confine themselves strictly to pharmaceutical business, but they are in the dwindling minority. It's the same way with the Press: it sells news more and more as a sideline, and attracts its customers mainly by its soda fountains, pipe-racks and "biologicals".

In spite of all the Press's claims and denials, it entertains more than it instructs—much, much more. It has far more in common with the entertainment business than with the educational system. This is true (at a glance) of the *Daily Mirror*; it is true (on second glance) of the *Manchester Guardian*; it is true of the Press as a whole. Entertain and instruct: the sugar pill. Each brand has a slightly different flavour, but if any one of them is taken daily for several months, a mild craving for it is gradually induced in the taker. This craving is sometimes mistaken and often advertised as "reader loyalty", and is frequently cited as showing the tremendous effectiveness of the pill. The actual effectiveness, however, remains open to question—as also the possibly harmful results to an addict of long standing. Though there is no known way of finding out for certain, it seems probable that the pill is neither very effective nor very harmful. Even when taken over a period of years, the effect on its addicts is apparently not fatal. The addiction is not incurable, though it is rarely cured. It is possible to lead a full life without reading a newspaper.

As you might expect, the pill-makers who admit that they are making sugar pills have succeeded in turning out a more cunningly blended and popular product, though it is not at all to the more cultivated taste, which prefers a certain grittiness and acidity. The popular Press knows that entertainment is its primary business, so it puts plenty of sugar in the well-tried formula, but includes some painless instruction as well. When the popular Press has something instructive to tell its readers it is careful to flatter their intelligence. The popular Press has become the great flatterer of the common man: it assures him every day how good he is, how right his prejudices are, how sound his head and heart, and how little anything matters that is outside his experience or understanding. It's rather like the morale-building machine once thought up by a light-hearted Government official: a mechanical hand to give encouraging pats on the back while a record in the mechanism repeated, "You're wonderful. You're wonderful."

The popular Press has at least partly dropped the pretence—and one of these days may drop it altogether—that it is primarily concerned to instruct: or even to tell the "news". As literacy spreads, standards in entertainment rise and standards in instruction fall. When the standards in both are about equal, and entertainment and instruction are on the same plane, the popular Press (or perhaps some pictorial equivalent of it) should have things all its own way.

The quality Press, on the other hand, will go to its grave refusing to admit that its purpose has anything whatever to do with entertainment. Some entertaining bits may have crept into their pages (Fourth Leaders, *dignified* gossip columns, autobiographical essays masquerading as sprightly reviews, etc.), but these are mere excrescences. No matter what may be said of the flibbertigibbet mass-circulation papers, they themselves are essentially solid, informative, instructive newspapers. That's their story, and they stick to it. But only a tiny minority of newspaper readers buy the quality papers, and only a minority of these readers accept them in the same solemn spirit in which they are offered. If the quality Press were read only by the people who believe that it's as necessary and important as it says it is, it would fail overnight. It has to have the support of readers who buy it not merely for instruction but for entertainment; because, in short, they like its flavour and are, however slightly, addicted to its mild effects.

I don't mean to say that these papers are not serious and usually high-minded enterprises, dedicated to the *res publica*, the best values of civilisation, etc., etc. I do mean to say that what attracts enough readers to keep them going is not their highmindedness but their sex appeal, however elegant, demure or angular. In other words, if they pretend they have nothing to do with the entertainment business they're talking through their hats, and a lot of their readers know better.

In a real democracy the Press can never be what Northcliffe and McCormick and all the other mad and power-hungry Press lords have tried to make it: a mere instrument of propaganda. Entertainment, in various crude and subtle forms, is always breaking in to spoil or weaken the effect. The Press of pure, distilled propaganda is only possible under dictatorship. If the precarious experiment of democracy fails—by turning itself into some form of Orwellian State, or is otherwise taken into the totalitarian camp—then the pill will be manufactured and issued by a Government monopoly, which will put no sugar on it whatever. Or the Press as such may be done away with, and some actual drug, like Aldous Huxley's "soma", mescalin or what-not, substituted for its soothing and stimulating function; while some even more painless and more effective form of mass instruction (perhaps a radio under the pillow) may take its place as public admonisher and instructor. Rather than submit to that Utopia, I'd fight for the *Daily Mirror* to the last barricade.

8

Our Press, the "best" and the "worst" of it, is a reflection of democratic culture because it's part of it. The Communists would say that it's a reflection *on* it, a complete giveaway of what a monkey-minded lot we really are. Communists pride themselves on taking a realistic view—we should often call it a statistical view—and therefore dismiss our quality Press as not worth considering, a mere corporal's guard alongside the swarming legions of the popular papers. It's a view shared by the popular Press itself and by the majority of newspaper readers. We don't have to agree that the quality Press is negligible, but if you count noses—and every nose in a democracy counts—we must admit that on this point the Communists are right. On balance, whether we like it or not, "the Press" is the popular Press. Must we also agree with the Communists that it not only shows us up but is helping to pull us down?

I was once staggered by a colleague of mine who said to me, quite casually and with an air of simply repeating a truism, that "journalism does more harm than good". I was too taken by surprise to argue, but I thought to myself: "Then why the hell are you here?" I had taken it for granted that journalism was a respectable job that could be done respectably. I decided he must be wrong. How could he be so sure? But then how could I be so sure either?

Was he right? It seems to me now that there are several answers. It is easier to see the harm journalism does, definite and indefinite, than the good it does, which is largely indefinite. It spreads despondency and alarm. It debases the general standard of taste. It hurts innocent bystanders. It talks too much. Such black marks the Press will have to accept. And on the good side? It tells us what is going on (but it tells us in a most contradictory and confusing way). It cheers us with good news (but how often the news is false). It popularises art, letters and science (and generally cheapens or misrepresents them in the process).

On the whole, it has often seemed to me that the worst thing about the Press is its talking too much. It could certainly do a better job if it were more occasional, less incessant. The ears of newspaper readers have become so hardened to the daily cry of "Wolf!" that when a wife asks her husband "What's in the paper?" nine times out of ten he will answer, "Oh, nothing." He won't have read the paper, of course, although he will think he has. What he has done is to look at his favourite features and skim the headlines in a dreamy way; one or two of them may have tripped his attention into reading the lead paragraph below it. Two or three things he sees may irritate, amuse or shock him. And that is called (by the Press) informing the public! A good deal of the time the public isn't even very much entertained; they're just reading the paper, because they're used to reading the paper. For once it's possible to agree with Northcliffe, or nearly agree: he said that the only two reasons people had for reading a newspaper were curiosity or habit. There are other reasons, of course, but curiosity and habit are enough excuse for most newspaper readers, most of the time.

The public would be better off reading books? Probably they would. But the public don't read books; they read newspapers. The question is: Does newspaper reading do more harm than good? After breathing this problem in and out for some ten years, it's my considered opinion that my colleague was right, in this sense: that if newspaper readers actually do read their papers thoroughly and pay strict attention to everything they read, the result is harmful because it increases the time-consuming chaos of their lives—which heaven knows are already muddled and wasteful enough. But he was wrong, in this sense: people don't read newspapers that way; they skip and skim, and therefore the Press simply shouldn't be taken as seriously as he took it, or as it takes itself. Newspaper readers themselves don't take the Press so seriously. They don't mistake it for a dangerous poison or for the elixir of life; they know it for what it is: a sugar pill.

I shall be accused of flippancy. I shall be told that the Press is a serious matter. It is, in some ways. Anyone who has been run over by a newspaper can tell you it's a very unpleasant, bruising and sometimes even crippling experience, but not fatal, or our public figures would keel over much more frequently than they do. Sometimes the Press hits the right rascal or uncovers a real den of thieves; and its "eternal vigilance" must be thanked for alerting us to some public dangers. But aside from this watchfulness, and its ever-changing exhibition of instructive facts and entertaining figures, the chief use of the Press is to supply the raw material for gossip. Newspapers are the main source of the "facts" that feed the beery arguments in the public bar, the laying-down of the law in clubs, the clack around the tea table, the slow exchanges at the farm gate. The Press can only pile up the midden; it's the readers who fork it around. Thus word of mouth still does more than the Press can.

9

The power and the glory of the Press are based on the false assumption that the best way to talk to a man is through a loudspeaker. It's certainly not the only way; but if you think of men as indistinguishable units of a group, community, newspaper circulation or concentration camp, this scattergun broadcasting may make some simple announcement understood. But a free Press doesn't make simple announcements. The Russian doctrinaires have tried to prove that men can be taught to forget that they are first and foremost individuals, or at least to act as if they had forgotten; and their Press is just the ticket for mass men. Our world is perhaps not so far ahead of the Russian doctrine as we like to suppose, but in theory at least we still honour the individual. Even the popular Press, which devoutly believes in the loudspeaker and the fullness thereof and talks to its mass audience in simple, shouted words, must continually flatter, woo and entertain its listeners to keep them from drifting off to listen to somebody louder. And, far from toeing one official line, our Press runs a continual Caucus Race of bewildering variety and contradiction. When the *Daily Mail* says "Yes," the *Mirror* yells "No!" and the *Times* lifts a disgusted eyebrow or murmurs, "It's really not like that at all." As long as the Press itself consists of newspapers with strongly individual personalities, this vital flaw (or democratic virtue) of contrariety guarantees us against the menace of an exclusively mass Press.

Meantime the Press does some good, some harm, but not nearly so much of either as is popularly supposed or as the Press would like us to think. It has some power, but not much; and its saving grace is to remind us that the variety of life is infinite and spiced with contradictions. (Even the captive Press of Russia, an inanimate instrument which must keep on asserting that there is no colour but red, ends by rousing a suspicion of redness and a desire for other colours.) Our Press is out to instruct us, so it says; we read it because we like gossip, in various forms—"news", rumours, and even false rumours. We are all addicted to the sugar pill: we have a sweet tooth or we like the after-taste or simply the glum comfort of a hard, round, vanishing feeling against the tongue. But is it necessary?

To the Editor of the *Times*, and also no doubt to most *Times* readers, this would be a ridiculous or outrageous question. There are other newspapers, or so-called newspapers, which need not be named, that would never be missed, in fact the country would be much better off without them. But the *Times* . . . And no doubt every editor of every paper, in his own guarded or misguided way, would say or think much the same. This would add up to a unanimous agreement, by the Press, that the Press is necessary. But would there be unanimous agreement among their readers? Suppose an honest plebiscite could be taken of Britain's 37 million newspaper readers.[1] In a way, partial plebiscites on the necessity of the Press have been taken: in the spring of 1955, for example, when a strike shut down all the London newspapers for more than three weeks, and millions of addicts were deprived of their daily dose. Life went on, but rather more quietly than usual. More people listened to the news bulletins on the wireless, which duly reported Churchill's resignation as Prime Minister (the only event I can remember from that "newsless" time). It appeared that the chief sufferers were some business firms which had to postpone publication of certain legal notices, and the newspapers themselves, which lost advertising revenue and money from daily sales. When the papers appeared again, everyone was glad to see them, of course—but the public calmness both during and after the strike was remarkable. I don't think it's an exaggeration to say that it was beginning to seem quite possible to get along comfortably without newspapers, and that if the strike had gone on just a few more weeks we might have got used to doing without them altogether.

The good that newspapers do, the harm they do, the necessity for them are all much exaggerated. They are in a sense the eyes of a community, but their eyesight is often astigmatic, myopic, colour-blind, or in other ways unreliable. They sometimes seem to be fomenting bad feeling and worse behaviour, but their direct influence on manners and morals is much feebler than it is touted to be: they are in fact not so much influential as representative. And we don't actually need them nearly so much as they say we do or as we like to think: the useful information they publish could be and often is circulated quite as effectively in other ways. Furthermore, we don't take our little daily dose of "news", when we get it, half as seriously as we pretend to.

I can understand how a young man would gladly give his

[1] An unlikely supposition, for two reasons: 1) there are still, I hope, several million Britons who resent being pried into and would refuse to answer; 2) a great many would probably say they thought the Press necessary, because they're addicted to reading a newspaper.

eyeteeth for a job on the *Guardian*. And for a job on the *Mirror*? Well, maybe one eyetooth. I'm sure it's a lot of fun to work on the *Mirror*, but on the *Guardian* I think there's more and better fun. Nearly any work is good work if you like it and can do it well and won't be arrested for doing it. The all-out effort that goes into a great many jobs is as near the act of poetry as most of us will get, however prosaic the result turns out to be. The best thing about a newspaper is the good work that goes into it.

APPENDIX A

CONTENTS OF THE *DAILY MIRROR* FOR MONDAY, FEBRUARY 11, 1957

(Stories marked with * appear in both the *Mirror* and the *Guardian*)

Number of pages: 20
Space taken up by pictures: 21%
Space taken up by advertisements: 32%
Editorial text: 47%

Front Page

In upper left-hand corner the standing head, *Daily Mirror*, printed in red; next to it the date and price, 2d.; under it the *Mirror's* slogan, FORWARD WITH THE PEOPLE, and the number of the issue, 16,536.

The rest of the page taken up by one story with two accompanying photographs, one of the Queen at Hurst Park races, the other of the Duke of Edinburgh at a football match at Gibraltar. Headlines and lead paragraphs:

** The Palace denies Royal rift*

FLY HOME, PHILIP!

The way to kill a silly rumour

Commander Richard Colville, the Queen's Press Secretary, confirmed to the *Daily Mirror* yesterday that he had had to take the extraordinary step of denying rumours of discord in the Royal Family.

He said he told an American news agency: "It is quite untrue that there is any rift between the Queen and the Duke of Edinburgh."

This denial follows widespread reports in American newspapers of rumours about the Queen and her husband.

These rumours are ridiculous and baseless.

. . . There is one simple way to scotch these malicious rumours.

LET THE DUKE FLY HOME TODAY TO JOIN THE QUEEN AND THEIR CHILDREN. THE ROYAL COUPLE CAN THEN SET OFF TOGETHER FOR PORTUGAL NEXT SATURDAY.

One advertisement: a powder to abate soot (sprinkle it on the fire).

Page 2

continued FLY HOME, PHILIP! for a column, ending

THEY SHOULD FLY

PHILIP HOME NOW

A feature story, by Frank Entwisle, told about weekend miners who dig for gold in Wales. Headline: *GOLD! They hope to hit the jackpot in Wales . . .* (The story reported that as yet the prospectors had not made enough to cover expenses.)

Viewpoint, one of the paper's two departments that print letters from readers, contained four letters:

1) H.T. said he had seen a clippie (woman bus conductor) on a bus in the busy City, knitting.

2) G.S.L. said he had worn a carnation every day since he came out of the Army in 1919.

3) Mrs. Moore Romford wanted stag hunting stopped; an official of the League Against Cruel Sports replied that a Bill to abolish it had often been introduced into Parliament but had never got beyond a second reading.

4) "Manageress" of a tobacco shop denied that shopkeepers were to blame for teen-age smokers.

One advertisement: dog food.

Page 3

Seven news stories:

1) *This little bull rocks the Rock*, a despatch from Gibraltar by Howard Johnson, the *Mirror's* chief reporter, announced that the Governor's cow had given birth to a calf and that "people here were a bit shaken at the news", because there is no bull in Gibraltar. It turned out that the cow had been taken to a Spanish bull, five miles across the frontier. An accompanying photograph showed the cow, her calf, and the Seaforth Highlander who takes care of her.

2) ANTHONY, 12, ALERTS THE YARD!: a boy had accidentally set off a burglar alarm in his home directly connected to Scotland Yard.

3) TRAGEDY AT DAWN: two soldiers and two girls in a car hit a lamp standard on the Great West Road, and one of the girls was killed.

4) GIRL DIES AT CLUB: the body of a 19-year-old German girl was found in her gas filled bedroom at the club where she had just come to work as a maid.

* 5) *The baby who fell* 50 *feet and lived*: an 18-month-old baby was found lying on soft ground, having apparently fallen from a third-storey window, with no injuries except a bloody nose.

* 6) RAIL CRASH MAN IS FOUND DEAD: the body of an engine-driver, killed in a collision two days earlier, had now been dug out of the wreckage.

7) A *Mirror* "Brief": Lord Grey de Ruthyn, 73, is becoming patron of the Derbyshire rock 'n' roll group.

Two advertisements: 1) Maternity clothes.
2) An antiseptic.

Page 4

Cassandra's column covered three topics: 1) Army stockpiling of ridiculous numbers of ridiculous objects; 2) the resignation of Lieut.-Commander Michael Parker, because of his divorce, from the Royal Household—"in places such as Cairo and Moscow, this hullabaloo . . . must have seemed one further proof of the convulsive idiocy of a dying Empire"; 3) Arlene Dahl, the Hollywood actress, solemnly describing the right and graceful way of sitting down.

One news story: * HUNTED GIRL GIVES HERSELF UP told of a young woman, recently released from a mental hospital, who had disappeared from home for a week and then gave herself up at a police station.

Two advertisements: 1) A tonic for babies.
2) A patent medicine for indigestion.

Page 5

A cartoon, *Useless Eustace*, showing him pulling down the dress of a large woman with whom he is having dinner. Caption: "Sorry! I thought I was pulling down the table cloth!"

Three news stories:

1) SOCCER FAN MIKE (only three) HAS TO GO: a little boy whose family lived near a football field gate-crashed a game on Saturday. His frantic mother called the police, who finally found him.

* 2) P.C. SHOT DOWN AS HE RIDES BIKE: a policeman in Dumfries, bicycling to investigate an attempted burglary, was

fired on from the doorway of a gunsmith's shop and hit three times. "A man was detained."

3) *The hound that went hareless*: one of a pack of harriers always quit as soon as he picked up the scent of a hare; the Master of the Hunt sentenced him to death but instead sold him to a man who wanted a pet.

Two advertisements: 1) A soap-powder.
2) A cough-drop.

Page 6

Six news stories:

1) NO-PETROL CAR LEFT ON BRIDGE for 5 days: a Jaguar, abandoned on Blackfriars Bridge in London, with a notice on its steering wheel "Run out of petrol", was towed away by the police. The owner's address was traced, but neighbours said he had gone to Scotland.

* 2) GIRL ON HORSE IS SHOT IN THE BACK: a 17-year-old girl in Yorkshire stopped her horse to give directions to two men on a motor-cycle; one of them carried a shotgun. As she moved off she heard a shot, was hit by two pellets in her back, and her horse bolted.

3) SCREAMS IN THE NIGHT: In Paris two airport hostesses, hearing screams coming from the darkened cabin of a plane that had recently landed, opened the cabin door and were set upon by 300 monkeys.

4) LIZ IN HOSPITAL: Elizabeth Taylor, the film actress, returned from her Mexican honeymoon and went into hospital for a back injury.

5) *Her life begins at 18 . . .* : A girl born with a hole in her heart that had kept her an invalid was successfully operated on and now looked forward to a normal life.

* 6) *VIRGINIA'S THE TOP ACTRESS:* Virginia McKenna was named by the British Film Academy the best British actress of 1956.

Four advertisements: 1) Caramels.
2) Patent medicine for indigestion.
3) Mattress, sheets and bedspreads.
4) A barley water.

Page 7

Three news stories:

* 1) *Two boys die in hole like an animal trap:* Somebody had removed one of the wooden man-hole covers over an underground reservoir in Lancaster and covered the opening with branches and twigs. A small boy fell in and drowned. Later his older cousin, who was looking for him, fell through the same opening, under the eyes of his mother. Both bodies were recovered. A photograph with the story showed both boys' smiling faces.

2) GUARD OF HONOUR FOR A PUP: A poodle puppy, a gift from a London housewife to Ulanova, prima ballerina of the Bolshoi Ballet, was met at Moscow airport by Ulanova and five officials.

3) A *Mirror* "Brief": American airmen's wives living in Britain are shown a U.S. Government film that advises them: "DON'T be condescending; DON'T be phoney; DO dress simply and in good taste."

A photograph captioned *Speedman's bride* showed an American actress, Louise Cordier, who was to marry a British racing driver, Peter Collins, in Miami that day.

Two advertisements: 1) A carpet-sweeper.
2) Margarine.

Page 8

Half the page taken up by a daily feature headed LAUGHTER: nine picture jokes, all but one with captions.

Three advertisements:
1) Pre-shrunk overalls.
2) A woman's fur coat ("Beaver Lamb").
3) Oranges.

Page 9

A feature (Donald Zec's STAR TURN, gossip about actors and actresses), headed *Will WALTER lead AVA to the ALTAR?* Most of it was an interview with Walter Chiari, the Italian actor and latest "heart interest" of Ava Gardner ("his is the voice that made Ava quaver—and will probably take Walter to the altar").

Besides a small photograph of Donald Zec there was a slightly larger one of Walter Chiari and a big one of Giorgia Moll, a new actress who had just landed a leading part in a Hollywood picture, *The Quiet American.*

A simple verbal puzzle, headed TWISTWORDS.

One advertisement:
1) Boys' socks.

Page 10

Four news stories:

1) MAX WALL IS ORDERED TO REST: A comedian, Max Wall, had suddenly left the cast of *The Pajama Game* and was said to be under doctor's orders to take a complete rest. The story

implied there was more to it than that: Max had recently denied rumours of discord with his second wife, Jennifer. "Of course we have our little quarrels like any other married couple," he said. "Jennifer is a lovable child and we are very happy together. Any suggestion of a bust-up is quite without foundation." Accompanying photograph showed Max and Jennifer smiling happily after their wedding.

2) *He let his family die in car—Police*: When a car plunged into a river at Miami, Florida, 50-year-old Ralph Evans and another man escaped from it but Evans' young wife and five little children drowned.

3) PREMIER'S HOME FROM HOME: Mr. Harold Macmillan spent his 63rd birthday at his country house in Sussex, which he has decided to use instead of the Prime Minister's official country house, Chequers.

4) *Mirror* "Brief": Winners at a Birmingham whist drive were Mr. and Mrs. N. O. Trump.

Four advertisements:

1) A starch.
2) A want ad for skilled machinists.
3) Copies of *Daily Mirror* photos—4*s*. each.
4) Diamond rings on the hire-purchase plan.

Page 11

Entirely taken up by one photograph captioned THE BOYS IN CHURCH, showing four Teddy-boys going through the motions of singing a hymn. The caption explained that the picture had been printed in the *Mirror* some time before and was now reproduced because "it has become famous"; as one of the "British Press Pictures of the Year" then on exhibition in

London it had drawn particular comment from the *Manchester Guardian*, which said: "The picture is not only a piece of technical brilliance and very funny; it is also rather poignant."

Page 12

Two features:

1) *Is life so wonderful with the 'other woman'? NO! says THE HUSBAND WHO RAN AWAY . . .* (Conclusion): If you are chafing at the domestic reins and there's a girl in your office or factory who appears to hold the key to freedom think, think in good, solid, practical terms of what you will be sacrificing. *Is she worth it? Is ANYTHING worth it?* There's usually a good reason why one got married to a particular woman. Sometimes it gets lost in the passing of the years. But you will be surprised how quickly you recall all the things you valued in your wife—*after you've left her*. No, don't be a fool. Stay at home; there's no place quite like it.

2) START RIGHT WITH THE STARS (Astrology column): Sample—SCORPIO (Oct. 24-Nov. 22): Tackle any controversial issue today or Friday.

Five advertisements:

1) Lemon juice in a plastic container.
2) A shaving lotion.
3) A skin ointment.
4) A vitamin capsule.
5) A block of miscellaneous ads: Situations vacant, London Amusements, Personal. (Under "Miscellaneous": Homesick Britons need the "Overseas Daily Mirror and Sunday Pictorial.")

Page 13

Six strip cartoons:

Buck Ryan, adventures of a two-fisted detective.

Ruggles, a middle-aged, middle-class couple whose problems and attitude are common to millions of Britishers.

Belinda (see p. 77).

The Flutters, an endless skirmish conducted with hearty vulgarity in the war between the sexes.

Garth, a Superman.

Romeo Brown, semi-amorous adventures of a young detective who is more of a ladies' man.

Three advertisements:
1) Woman's suit with extra skirt.
2) Magazine of popular music.
3) A baby's soap.

Page 14

Live Letters, the second and more homely of the *Mirror's* two correspondence columns, "conducted by the Old Codgers", containing 9 letters, an "Od-ad" and "Today's Thought". Sample letters: "Waiting to catch my train on a busy main line station, I saw an irate business man hurry up to a ticket collector and snarl 'Hastings?' The ticket collector, with an innocent expression on his face, simply replied '1066, sir'. The 'tycoon' stamped off snapping: 'I can't wait that long—I want the 4.20.' " Comment of the Old Codgers: *Small wonder these business men get tetchy if they pack sixty-six minutes into every hour!*

Please tell us the length of the longest and second longest railway platforms in the world. *1. Sonepur, India: 2,415 ft. 2. Manchester Victoria and Exchange: 2,194 ft.*

Could you please confirm that the British Museum library is the largest one in the world? My brother disagrees. He reckons the biggest is the Library of Congress, in America.—*The Library of Congress it is, with more than 10,860,000 books and pamphlets. The British Museum contains between six and seven million.*

I wonder if other readers ever overhear fragments of conversation that puzzle them. The other morning I was passing a kitchen window when I heard someone say: 'Will you please remove your foot from the teapot? . . . —*Nothing peculiar about that remark, sir. We Old Pair get most annoyed when George tries the temperature of our cuppa with his big toe!*

Od-Ad: "Sale. Winter boys' pants." Old Codgers' comment: *Chilly mortals.*

Today's Thought: A truth that's told with bad intent beats all the lies you can invent—WILLIAM BLAKE.

A children's strip cartoon, *Sooty*, the adventures of a toy bear.

Three advertisements: 1) An insurance company.
2) A rum.
3) A cat food.

Page 15

The page (headed *Telepage*) taken up by news about television and radio programmes for the coming day and comment, mainly uncritical, on some programmes of the night before. Headline: HIDDEN 'MIKES' IN A CATHEDRAL . . . *For the enthroning of an Archbishop* referred to the first item, which told of the preparations in Westminster Cathedral for televising the enthronement of the Most Rev. William Godfrey as Roman Catholic Archbishop of Westminster. A separate column listed all TV and radio programmes scheduled for that day.

The only photograph was of a TV comedian part of whose stock-in-trade had been a beard; he was now clean-shaven.

Three advertisements: 1) Sweets.
2) A liniment.
3) A cigarette.

Pages 16-19

The *Mirror's* regular four Sport pages: first two on football, third on horse-racing, fourth a miscellany. The news stories reported results, sometimes in abbreviated summary, of games, matches and races, and gave inside gossip or speculation about various sports figures.

On *page 16* Tony Horstead gave six "stories behind Saturday's goals". Sample: Portsmouth were leading Chelsea, 2-1. Uprichard, Portsmouth's goalkeeper, seeing a linesman wave a flag and hearing a whistle, thought a foul had been called and momentarily turned his back, whereupon a Chelsea man scored. It was not the referee but someone in the crowd who had blown a whistle. Said Uprichard afterwards: "I wouldn't mind a couple of minutes with the chap who blew that whistle."

Also *Jane*, the *Mirror's* oldest and best-known strip cartoon. (In this instalment Jane was fully clothed, but about to disappear into a cubicle to change into the briefest of scanties.)

Two advertisements: 1) A stout.
2) A cough drop.

On *page 17*, nine stories about football, one (HARRIS WINS IN PARIS) about a professional cycling race, a list of the day's sport fixtures (soccer, rugger, table tennis and boxing) and a photograph captioned *Silent prayer?* showing the Charlton goalkeeper diving vainly to block a kick, his hands clasped and eyes downcast.

On *page 18*, two semi-news stories about race horses and their chances in forthcoming races (the Grand National, the Manifesto Stakes, the Stratford 'Chase, the Cymbeline 'Chase), a report of two horses which had run well in an Irish steeplechase, and two columns of esoteric information about horses entered in races for that day. Two photographs: one of a horse named Must, the other of a jockey named Billy Rees.

Also a crossword puzzle.

On *page 19*, five news stories:

1) STONE PUT THE SKIDS UNDER 'EM ALL reported a bicycle race in which the course was ankle-deep in mud, and in which the winner, Don Stone, fell twice.

* 2) *Ray's 99 foils M.C.C.:* the first innings of a cricket match between Griqualand West and the touring Marylebone Cricket Club, in Kimberley, South Africa.

3) GREAVES SINKS WALES: In a junior football match between England Youths and Wales Youths, Jimmy Greaves, England inside right, scored three goals. England beat Wales, 7-1.

* 4) CRUMP KEEPS KEY JOBS IN ATHLETICS: the British Amateur Athletic Board re-elected Jack Crump as Hon. Secretary and team manager, though after 20 years at the job he wanted to resign. The *Mirror* writer thought it a pity he wasn't allowed to.

* 5) *White Devils fried them to a frazzle:* England's gallant victory over Ireland in rugger, though they were a man short for most of the game, after an England forward broke a rib.

Tips on dog-racing (best bets on tonight's races).

Sports summary: results of matches in ice hockey, table tennis and lawn tennis.

Two photographs: one captioned HERE'S MUD IN YOUR EYE, showing Don Stone on his bicycle splashing through a mudhole; the other of Jack Crump.

Page 20

On this last page the *Mirror* repeats its standing head (*Daily Mirror*) but varies the accompanying slogan to THE BIGGEST DAILY SALE ON EARTH.

Under WORLD NEWS SPOTLIGHT (also a standing head) were the only three serious foreign news stories in this issue:

Two salvage ships leave—their Canal job is over: progress in the unblocking of the Suez Canal, an expected meeting of the U.N. General Assembly to discuss the Middle East, fears that Egypt may create further difficulties.

Wounded Briton shoots back: an unnamed British civilian in Cyprus, shot by gunmen in the shoulder, fired back at them as they ran away.

* *The Communists lose an ally:* Nenni's Italian Socialist Party, meeting at Venice, decided to break with the Communists.

Four other news stories:

1) SCARED GIRL TELLS OF DEATH THREAT: in London a young Latvian woman, a political refugee, asked for police protection, saying that a man, whose name she gave the police, had threatened to kill her. The body of a young man, also a Latvian, had been found on a lonely heath in Kent. He had been a friend of the girl's, and she thought he had been killed by the man who threatened her.

2) ANGER OVER RENT BILL ALARMS TORY M.PS.: A Government Bill to remove rent restrictions was, according to the *Mirror*, rousing wide and deep resentment among the "middle class", and might even bring on a General Election.

3) *Father of three dies in mystery gas trap:* in Sweden, five engineers were asphyxiated by lethal gas in the boiler room of an iron foundry. "One of those killed was a Briton. . . . The other four were Swedes."

4) SERENADE TO BILL HALEY: 1,500 teen-age fans gathered

outside a Coventry hotel where Bill Haley and his band (of rock 'n' roll fame) were staying overnight, and chanted "We want Bill." Haley finally appeared on a balcony, and commented: "Terrific."

A full-length photograph of Princess Grace (Kelly) of Monaco, captioned *PRINCESS GRACE STEPS OUT,* showed her leaving Monaco Cathedral, in green turban hat and mink coat, after a thanksgiving service for the birth of her daughter.

In the blank space reserved for Stop Press (last-minute bulletins): the weather report for the day, printed sideways.

One advertisement: Port.

APPENDIX B

CONTENTS OF THE *MANCHESTER GUARDIAN* FOR MONDAY, FEBRUARY 11, 1957

Number of pages: 14
Space taken up by pictures: 4·6%
Space taken up by advertisements: 46·7%
Editorial text: 48·7%

Front Page

At top of page, centred, the standing head MANCHESTER GUARDIAN: under it the number of the issue, 34,407, four stars (showing that this is the second or London edition). The date, and the price, 3*d.*

Fourteen news stories:

1) MR. SANDYS TO MEET GEN. NORSTAD: Speculation from "Our Correspondent" in Paris on what the new American commander of S.H.A.P.E. might say to Duncan Sandys, Britain's Minister of Defence; "it is believed here that if General Norstad finds the British Government adamant in their decision to effect defence economies, he will urge that they should be made in the R.A.F. and above all in the Royal Navy."

2) BEST—OR WORST—ABOUT RATES AND DEFENCE THIS WEEK: More speculation, from "our Political Correspondent", on two promised statements of Government policy. If the Minister of Housing "is able to promise tomorrow that the Government accepts the principle of abolishing or reducing industrial de-rating, that would be some comfort to rate-payers . . ." and

"Mr. Sandy's statements in the defence debate on Wednesday may promise savings in national expenditure on a scale which, ultimately, would bring greater tax relief . . . ."

3) EIGHTH BY-ELECTION: The death of Sir David Gammans, Conservative M.P. for Hornsey, will necessitate another by-election.

4) U.S. IN QUANDARY ON SANCTIONS: a Washington despatch from Max Freedman reported that the possibility of the U.N.'s applying sanctions against Israel "has confronted the Eisenhower Administration with four problems" (and listed them).

5) OIL FOR EGYPT DELAYED: a Reuter's despatch reported that the first commercial vessel to enter the Suez Canal since it was blocked had found itself blocked at Ismailia.

6) APPOINTMENT TO N.C.B. CRITICISED: A mineworkers' union had protested the appointment of Mr. James Crawford to the National Coal Board, on the ground that he had "no mining industry background". He was president of the National Union of Boot and Shoe Operatives.

7) 'PRAVDA' LEAVES IT LATE: Victor Zorza reported that a letter to *Pravda* from five M.Ps. about Hungary had finally been printed in *Pravda*, with comments, 44 days after it was sent.

8) BOMBS IN CROWDED STADIUMS: a Reuter's despatch from Algiers reported the explosion of two bombs in sports stadiums there, killing 11 and injuring 45.

* 9) BODY OF SECOND BOY FOUND: "our Special Correspondent" reported from Lancaster (in much greater detail than the account in the *Mirror*) the story of the two boys who drowned in an underground reservoir. The *Guardian* reporter made no implication that a manhole cover had been removed and the opening camouflaged with branches; he did say "the woodwork of one of the covers, opened today to admit the frogmen, seemed to me rotten to a sponge-like degree."

10) INVITATION STILL OPEN: "our Diplomatic Correspondent" reported that Mr. Bulganin had renewed his invitation to the

Prime Minister to visit Moscow in May, or later. "Conceivably the Soviet leaders feel that, if they could persuade Mr. Macmillan to go to Moscow after his visit to Washington, they might be able to sow new seeds of discord in the re-established Anglo-American relations."

11) ADEN VILLAGE TO BE DESTROYED: a Reuter's despatch said that villagers of Danaba had been warned that the village will be destroyed unless dissident tribesmen are handed over to the authorities.

12) AMERICAN PRESS FINDS A ROYAL "RIFT": Alistair Cooke reported from New York the furor in the U.S. tabloid Press over a story, "first cabled to this country by the *Baltimore Sun's* London bureau", of a "rift" in the marriage of the Queen and the Duke of Edinburgh. Cooke concluded: "It is the obvious, if sad, obligation of a reporter surely to report the 'news' that monopolises the front pages and obsesses a continent, even if it is no news at all."

* 13) PALACE SPOKESMAN'S DOUBLE DENIAL: "our London Staff" added a footnote that the *Baltimore Sun* staff writer who had sent the first report was Miss Joan Graham. Her report had said that "unidentified members of cafe society in London were 'talking openly of a rift'."

14) MR. DE VALERA TO VISIT BELFAST: "our Political Correspondent" noted that the Leader of the Opposition in the Republic of Ireland would visit Belfast, to take part in a debate on the U.N., for the first time since 1929.

One photograph: of a police frogman about to enter the underground reservoir at Lancaster.

Three advertisements:
1) Corrugated steel.
2) A mission for needy children.
3) Movable steel partitions.

Page 2

Four news stories:

1) TEACHERS GROPING FOR UNITY: "our Local Government Correspondent" reported the points brought up in speeches and debates at a meeting of the London Teachers' Association.

2) FORD TO MAKE LORRIES IN BRAZIL: a British United Press despatch from Rio de Janeiro said that the Ford Motor Company of Brazil planned to make lorries at its Sao Paulo plant.

3) STUDENTS MAY NOT LIVE IN FLATS: "our Correspondent" wrote that Nottingham University would keep the rule forbidding unmarried students to live in flats which have no resident landlady.

4) DINING-CAR STAFFS PROTEST: Union officials met in Manchester to protest a statement that "embezzling in railway dining-cars is becoming such a grave position that the receipts are right down and we are running at a loss".

Three obituaries: Admiral Nicholas Horthy, former Regent of Hungary.
Sir David Gammans, Conservative M.P.
Mr. J. D. Mack, former Labour M.P.

Feature story on Motoring (weekly feature), A NEW CHALLENGE FROM ABROAD: describing the B.M.W. Isetta, the latest German import in the miniature car field, with criticism (generally favourable) of its points and petrol consumption ("driven hard", 75 miles to the gallon).

A MOTORING DIARY: minor notes on motoring; this one mildly expressing the wish that "the manifold authorities which are allowed to dig holes in roads would take rather more care to restore the surface when they have finished digging their hole."

Three letters from motoring readers.

Three photographs, showing the stripped-down chassis, interior and outside of an Isetta.

Eight advertisements:
1) A block of 16 "Personals".
2) A motor-scooter.
3) A car-hire firm.
4) A small foreign car.
5) Another small foreign car.
6) A restaurant.
7) A British car.
8) Leather upholstery.

Page 3

A full-page advertisement for an industrial group.

Page 4

Headed *Mainly for Women.* Three feature stories:

1) SOME REFLECTIONS ON POLIO, by a Patient (a man), gave a completely unsentimental account of what it is like to become a cripple. Most sustaining assets: a wife, new-found interests, an adequate income, memories.

2) THE JUMPING SETTEE, by Mary Taylor, recited the advantages of having one piece of furniture the children are allowed to jump on.

3) IN THE KITCHEN, initialled B.D.B., gave some labour-saving hints for housewives.

One letter, headed TOO MUCH FASHION?, criticised the "intensive coverage" of fashion shows in the *Guardian*, and pleaded for more "in this reputable paper" about women's more serious business.

One news story: SCHOOL STANDARDS IN JAPAN, a despatch from Hessell Tiltman in Tokyo, reported that a test among primary and high school students in Japan indicated that teaching methods of language and mathematics left something to be desired.

One photograph: a model wearing a short-sleeved jumper.

Seven advertisements:
1) A stout.
2) A fur remodeller.
3) Switzerland.
4) Sheets.
5) Insulation against draughts.
6) A Commonwealth airline.
7) Cigarettes.

Page 5

Three news stories:

1) STEADY DEMAND FOR FACSIMILE OF LINDISFARNE GOSPELS, from "our Special Correspondent" in Birmingham, reported that a limited edition of 680 copies, at £122 a copy, was selling briskly: and told in some detail the history of the Lindisfarne Gospels—written in Latin about 724 and later glossed between the lines in Anglo-Saxon.

* 2) FILM OF THE YEAR: the British Film Academy award for the best moving picture of 1956 went to the French *Gervaise*; the best British film, *Reach for the Sky*.

3) UNIVERSITY NEWS listed the latest appointments and scholarship-winners at Cambridge and at the University College of North Wales.

Three feature stories:

MISCELLANY, a daily department of lighter-veined paragraphs, contained four, two of which were concerned with a deep-voiced Victorian singer, Samuel Slack of Tideswell. The Duchess of Devonshire, who campaigned against the cruel sport of bull-baiting, once thought she heard a bull in torment but discovered that the noise was Samuel Slack, singing; she thereupon paid for his tuition and furthered his career.

THE ABADAN RUN, by Leslie A. Rocker, told calmly of the horrors of life aboard a British tanker plying between the Persian Gulf and Australia; in the incessant heat of the Gulf "the ship became a floating oven. The metal absorbed so much heat that to touch parts of it during the day burnt the skin. The fresh water, stored in tanks on an upper deck, was often too hot to use for washing and salt water was used instead. Shaving, of faces never completely dry, left the skin raw and tender. The ice-water tap was unlocked for brief periods only. . . ."

NO TRUMPETS HERE, by Roger Lloyd, complained that he had just read four books on theology, all badly written. He suggested that theologians should pattern themselves on a Victorian scholar, J. R. Illingworth, who "would decide what he wanted his next paragraph to say and then he would write it. Then he read it to himself and removed, translated, or explained every technical term. Then he read it aloud, generally to his wife, and between them they would get rid of the long words, and polish the sentences till they sang with prose rhythm."

Two reviews:

1) KIRSTEN FLAGSTAD IN "ALCESTE", by Edward Greenfield, reviewed an album of Flagstad records, made after her retirement. "The nobility, richness and power that made Flagstad's voice so unique are still there in full measure."

2) TRADITION AND TALENT, by Eric Newton, reviewed an exhibition of painting and sculpture by the Camberwell School of Arts and Crafts in London, and agreed with Lord David Cecil (who opened the exhibition) that "a tradition with a firm classical basis need not be dull."

NEW REQUIEM AT THE "THREE CHOIRS" announced that

Julius Harrison's new Requiem would be included in the programmes of the Three Choirs Festival, to be held at Worcester in September.

BOOKS RECEIVED by the *Guardian* listed 17 titles.

Two photographs: details from a page of the Lindisfarne Gospels, and Professor Alan S. C. Ross of Birmingham University, one of the editors, working at the text.

Two advertisements: 1) An automatic boiler control.
2) Listing of London theatres, opera, art exhibitions, etc., also in Manchester and Liverpool.

Page 6 (Leader page)

Four leaders:

1) BIGGER RISKS, apropos the day's meeting between General Norstad and Mr. Sandys, recapitulated the Western strategic position in Europe and of Britain in particular, and pointed out that "as defence turns more to missiles and less to men . . . so Britain becomes a more marked target." And as air bases in Britain are converted or new ones built for launching long-range rockets, these will become primary targets for Russia; "since their exact location may be hard to pinpoint, hydrogen bombs may be used against them rather in the manner of fly-swatters." Calling these prospects "a grim undertaking . . . but probably the best way out", the *Guardian* suggested an additional dispersal of launching sites to "the Arctic islands, Cyprus, and points farther east . . . ".

2) *Brainstorms*, commenting on the fuss kicked up in the American Press over rumours of a "rift" in the Royal Family, pointed out that the rumours fell flat in Britain: "the report was too fantastic to be worth bothering with."

3) *Bans and Restraints* noted that "the Roman Catholic Church still wealds [sic] the weapon of the Index"; two books by Unamuno have just been put on the banned list. And in France "La Vie Intellectuelle", a Dominican periodical, "has just very abruptly ceased publication."

4) *The Obsessed* applauded a new book by Professor Edward Shils of Chicago, whose point was that Americans have recently been obsessed "not so much with real security as with 'secrets which could not be kept' and 'secrets which need not be kept'. The sickness in America has abated since 1954—and this bears witness to the steadiness of American society, but the wounds will take time to knit."

Two news stories:

1) JEWISH POPULATION OF BRITAIN, a Reuter's despatch from New York, reported that Jews in Britain had increased since 1939 by 60,000, that over 7% of the world's Jewish population (11,810,000) lives in the British Commonwealth, nearly 50% (5,200,000) in the United States.

2) A short announcement (with no head) stated that the Queen and the Duke of Edinburgh would pay an official visit to Norwich on July 3.

Three features:

1) *Our London Correspondence* (daily), contained seven paragraphs. Two called attention to that evening's dinner of the English Speaking Union, at which General Norstad and the Prime Minister would both speak (General Norstad would probably insist that N.A.T.O.'s forces must not be weakened). One paragraph described small boys trying to get autographs from football players; another reported a loud but orderly procession of 300 Pakistanis protesting against India's treatment of Kashmir; two paragraphs considered the probable outcome of the forthcoming by-election at Hornsey; the last applauded an English version of Rigoletto just produced by Sadler's Wells.

"The audience responded heartily, clapping at all the best places."

2) A COUNTRY DIARY (daily feature), from Westmorland, initialled A.H.G., deplored the decline in slate quarrying there. "A fine local industry with long traditions is being slowly strangled . . . " because "youngsters in the dales don't go in for quarrying nowadays . . .".

3) INLAND TRANSPORT IN WAR, initialled J.R.L.A., reviewing a volume on wartime inland transport in Britain, called it "an admirable record of what was achieved during the war, but its real importance is in questioning assumptions about transport that are still taken for granted." The "dangerous myth" that British railways had plenty of surplus capacity had resulted in massive piling up of goods, long delays, cargoes held up, ships kept waiting, "appalling congestion".

Six *Letters to the Editor* commented on: India and Kashmir, Britain's housing problem, the Turkish claim to Cyprus, the inequity of U.N. edicts (peremptory to Israel, ignored by Egypt), the unjust treatment by Germany of anti-Nazi Germans, the "vicious smear" of the Royal Household in a recent cartoon by Low, which "even makes offensive reference to the Royal Family's well known affection for dogs". This last, signed by J. A. Leavey and sent from the House of Commons, was answered by Ed. "Guardian": "To say that Low's cartoon 'viciously smears' the Royal Household and others is surely unwarranted. The Victorians at least were not so squeamish".

One advertisement: A Manchester department store.

Page 7

Fourteen news stories:

1) ULBRICHT CONFIRMED IN POWER, from Terence Prittie at Bonn, reported further signs of East Germany's difficulties—a

shortage of coalminers, student disorders at Dresden, Halle and East Berlin over the Hungarian situation. Prittie wrote that "the East German regime is marking time, at Moscow's orders", and that Walter Ulbricht, the key man in the East German Government, "will remain Moscow's faithful instrument".

2) FORTY TRIBESMEN TO DIE: the Supreme Court at Wewak, New Guinea, has sentenced 40 tribesmen to death for the massacre of 29 members of another tribe last August.

3) AMERICAN ROAD TO SOCIALISM?, from Alistair Cooke in New York, reported the meeting of the U.S. Communist party in its first national convention since 1950. There were deep divisions. A letter from Jacques Duclos, French Communist, containing "a studied rebuke" to the U.S. party for "dangerous tendencies", was meekly accepted by William Foster, the ageing party chairman, but not by Eugene Dennis, the secretary; Howard Fast, the most prolific propagandist of U.S. Communism, resigned from the party. "The comrades could find no hotel in the city that would house them. They met in an old Russian Orthodox church."

4) POLAND DEVALUES ITS CURRENCY: but not enough, according to British and American business men. "One effect will be to make it cheaper for Westerners to visit Poland and six times dearer for Poles to visit or to telephone the West."

5) ARAB "SUMMIT" TALKS NEXT WEEK-END? King Saud of Saudi Arabia is expected to brief President Nasser, King Hussein of Jordan, and President Kuwatly of Syria on his recent talks with President Eisenhower, at a conference in Cairo.

6) AWARD TO NOVELIST: John dos Passos, for "a lasting contribution to American letters", was awarded a gold medal by the National Institute of Arts and Letters in New York.

7) POLAND DETAINS A BRITISH CITIZEN: A former British Army sergeant, Polish-born but now a British subject, made the

mistake of visiting relatives in Poland without first making sure he could get out again.

8) USE OF FORCE IN KASHMIR corrected an earlier report of what Mr. Krishna Menon had actually said about violence in Kashmir; he had blamed "tribes for whom Pakistan, and not India, was responsible".

9) CARIBBEAN CONSTITUTION: The draft of the Constitution for the West Indies Federation has been almost completed at Kingston, Jamaica.

10) END NEAR OF LONG GERMAN STRIKE: The metal workers' strike in Schleswig-Holstein, which has lasted 16 weeks, seems near a settlement.

11) COMMUNIST THREAT "INCREASING": In Washington, the House Committee on un-American Activities reported that the danger of Communism was increasing; that the "Fund for Freedom", financed by the Ford Foundation, was giving great aid and comfort to the Communists; and that the Soviet Union has "the equivalent of 20 army divisions engaged in propaganda, espionage, and subversion in the U.S."

12) *Foreign News in brief:* Five Jordanians to be hanged in Amman as Israeli spies; Miss Eartha Kitt, the singer, after dining with Mr. Nehru: "He is rather good-looking and interesting, very interesting;" etc.

* 13) NENNI'S SOCIALISTS DECIDE FOR UNITY: from "Our Special Correspondent" in Venice, reported the meeting of the Italian Socialist Congress and their decision to maintain absolute political independence "from any bonds with the Communist party".

14) CONDITIONS FOR KASHMIR TALKS: Mr. Nehru announced that he was willing to discuss Kashmir with Pakistan or anybody provided that two things were clearly understood—that Kashmir became a part of India in 1947, and that Pakistan had made an "unprovoked and improper invasion of Kashmir".

One photograph: The bay at Wiawera, on North Island, New Zealand, "where Sir Anthony and Lady Eden are to spend the first part of their holiday".

Three advertisements: 1) A hospital for the blind.
2) The Italian Riviera.
3) An instrument manufacturer.

Page 8 (*City page*)

Ten news stories:

1) PROSPECTS IN AUSTRALIA, by "Our Financial Staff", said it was time to make a new assessment of the Australian market, "the largest and the most mercurial of all the markets open to the British exporter. . . . It looks as if the Australian market in 1957 may be less easy than in former years, but perhaps for this reason it may be more firmly based."

2) COMPANY AFFAIRS: listed news of six different companies.

3) THE MONEY MARKET: "Money was short in Lombard Street on Saturday and official help was given."

4) FOREIGN EXCHANGES: "quiet but firm".

5) RAW COTTON TRADE: from "a Cotton Trade Correspondent", reported that trading in futures has again been "very circumscribed" this week.

6) HIGHER FREIGHT RATES TO SOUTH AFRICA: up 7½% from Friday next.

7) BUSINESS NEWS IN BRIEF: chiefly personnel changes in various companies.

8) MICHAEL NAIRN & GREENWICH LIMITED: report of the annual meeting of a linoleum company.

9) DISTRICT BANK LIMITED: 127th annual meeting, very briefly reported.

10) SCOTER NESTS IN ENGLAND: from "a Correspondent", reported that the grey phalarope and the long-tailed duck had joined the list of migratory visitors, and that last year, for the first time, the scoter (a sea-duck) had made its first successful nesting in England in modern times.

PROGRESS AND PROFITS: trade notes on the textile industries.

One chart: showing American cotton futures at Liverpool.

Four lists: Fish prices, foreign bank rates, Egyptian and Indian cotton markets.

The full text of *Pravda's* reply to the letter from five M.Ps.

Four advertisements:
1) A bank.
2) A teleprinter service.
3) Job wanted by "top-level sales engineer."
4) Electrical company stock.

Page 9

Five news stories:

1) EXPANDING THE ECONOMY reported excerpts from week-end speeches of four politicians. Chief place was given to Mr. Jo Grimond, M.P., Leader of the Parliamentary Liberal party, who said that Britain could only develop an expanding economy as part of a united Continent or a Commonwealth which included East Africa and Canada.

2) JOHN KAY'S COTTAGE SAVED: the decaying Lancashire birth-place of one of its "most illustrious sons, the man who revolutionised the cotton industry" by inventing the flying shuttle in 1773, has been bought, renovated and will be used as a private dwelling.

3) VEHICLE BUILDERS BAN OVERTIME: a Birmingham union of

vehicle builders, worried by unemployment in the industry, has instructed its members not to work overtime.

4) EXETER UNIVERSITY SCHEME: a building and development programme for the university will provide several new buildings before 1960.

5) HUNGARIANS REFUSED AT TWO PITS: 1,600 miners at a colliery near Doncaster voted against accepting Hungarian workers (five years ago they had banned Italians); 2,200 miners at a near-by colliery did the same.

One advertisement (filling 6/7ths of the page): a stock issue of shares in a limited stock company.

Page 10 (Sports)

Fifteen news stories:

* 1) GALLANT ENGLISH PACK DRAW IRELAND'S STING, from Larry Montague, gave a much more detailed account than the *Mirror's* of the International rugby match between England and Ireland, and noted the partisanship of the Dublin spectators: an "inevitable penalty was greeted with howls and whistles of rage by a crowd which already had been exasperated by its own side's failures and had now decided that it did not like the referee either."

2) NAVY PUT LIMITED CHANCES TO GOOD USE, from "our Special Correspondent", gave a run-of-the-mine report of a run-of-the-mine rugby match.

3) SPLENDID EFFORT BY HEATLEY, from "a Special Correspondent", reported a cross-country race under soggy conditions: "There were long stretches of plough and sown land, ditches that were full and grassland that squelched to the tread."

4) SPORTS NEWS IN BRIEF: five items, on rugby, cricket, squash rackets, football and a walking race.

* 5) ONE BATSMAN DEFIES M.C.C.: The cricket match at Kimberley, South Africa, still in progress.

6) HANDICAPPED WIGAN TEAM FIGHTS TO THE LAST: another rugby match in which one side lost a player through injury, played hard but lost, 11-13.

7) COMBINED SERVICES SCORE AN IMPRESSIVE VICTORY, from "our Hockey Correspondent", was a soberly expert account of a hockey match played by men.

8) SOUTH'S NARROW ESCAPE, from "a Special Correspondent", was much brighter reading about a much worse hockey match, played by women. The reporter showed how he felt about it in the very first sentence: "Driving down the valley of the Test, ruminating on the most fascinating sport of all with rain pelting down and water everywhere, it seemed impossible that the women's hockey match between South and West would be played at all." But it was. "As a game of hockey it need not live long in the memory . . . Hockey should be a game of skill, much of this was a game of chance."

9) MISS BUXTON LOSES: Miss A. Buxton, the British Wightman Cup player, lost in the final of the French covered court lawn tennis championships to Mrs. T. Long, of Australia.

10) ALL SWEETNESS AND LIGHT AT OLD TRAFFORD, by "an Old International", described a football match in which Manchester United beat Arsenal, 6-2. "What did cause 60,000 pairs of eyes to protrude like organ stops was the clowning that broke out immediately afterwards. . . ." The most thrilling goal of the match was made by Whelan. "Making a gate of his legs for Pegg's centre to pass through to Taylor, he wheeled about in time to receive Taylor's prompt return pass and brush it sideways into the Arsenal net as if it had been a piece of orange peel on the pavement."

11) FINE GOALKEEPING BY BOLLANDS, from "Silchester", reported a football match in which Tottenham Hotspur beat

Sunderland 5-2, "by virtue of greater determination and confidence rather than superior skill".

12) BISHOP AUCKLAND IN LAST EIGHT: an amateur football club which has reached the national finals in the past three seasons has now reached the last eight.

* 13) ADVISORY BODY TO BE FORMED: the Amateur Athletic Association has decided to set up an advisory committee, including representatives of active athletes and coaches. J. C. G. Crump was elected honorary secretary and team manager of the British Amateur Athletics Board.

14) RUGBY AND LACROSSE RESULTS: listed the scores of Saturday's rugby and lacrosse matches.

15) LEAGUE AND CLUB RESULTS: listed the scores of Saturday's professional and amateur football matches.

One photograph: of the break-away from a line-out in the rugby match between England and Ireland.

Page 11

One special article: THE ENGLAND OF SHAKESPEARE, DICKENS —AND INDIFFERENCE, by "Our Special Correspondent", described the plight of Egyptian refugees who are British subjects, many of whom had never seen England, could not speak English, had once been well off but were now possessionless. Said one of them (who could speak English eloquently): "I work for more than thirty years in Egypt and I accept charity from no one not ever. I do not wish to be on the shoulders of anybody."

Twelve news stories:

1) PATIENT CALLED BACK told how a loudspeaker at a football match summoned one of the spectators to return to the infirmary where he had had an anti-tetanus injection and should have waited for a nurse to test his reaction.

2) CHIEF CONSTABLE MAY APPEAL, so cautiously worded as to be nearly incomprehensible, seemed to indicate that the county police of Cardiganshire had been under inquiry, that the report had found "certain aspects" unsatisfactory and that the Chief Constable was considering an appeal.

3) CHURCHES AND RACIAL DISCRIMINATION: Canon Collins of St. Paul's told a Nottingham audience that if he were an African in Africa and not a Christian, he would become a Communist. "Where else can they turn?" he asked.

4) STUDENT IN CONCERT AT WEEK'S NOTICE: a 20-year-old girl had only a week to learn a soprano part in a Mahler symphony, but did it to the conductor's taste.

5) TALKS TO-DAY ON BRIGGS DISPUTE, by "our Industrial Staff", reported an effort to reinstate a shop steward whose dismissal had caused an unofficial strike that had shut the Briggs and Ford plants for two weeks.

6) AWARD FOR RESCUING CADET SHIP CREW: the Minister of Transport, Mr. Watkinson, presented a silver cigarette box to Captain Harry Cater, master of the freighter Clan Maclean, for rescuing the 23 members of the crew of the ketch Moyana last July.

7) ESTATE TO SELL 27,000 ACRES: Mr. J. Wyndham, of Petworth House, will sell 27,000 acres of his Sussex and Cumberland properties, to meet the death duties on the estate of his uncle, the late Lord Leconfield.

8) ARUNDEL CASTLE MAY PASS TO THE NATION: a personal bill, to come before the House of Lords in May, will preserve the Duke of Norfolk's castle "for the benefit of the nation" and as a residence for the Earl Marshal of England (the Duke of Norfolk).

9) INJUNCTION AGAINST SHAREHOLDERS: a knitwear firm was granted an injunction to prevent eight investment trust companies and five individual shareholders from voting at an extraordinary company meeting.

10) DRAWING-ROOM CATS WHICH NEVER PUT A PAW WRONG: by "our own Reporter", reported the championship show of the Lancashire and North-western Counties Cat Club. The reporter noted a marked distinction between the pedigreed cats and the others; but one in particular of the non-pedigreed caught his eye: "Joey looked very clean and very angry. When last seen he was being held up by his milkstained owner for a photograph, all four glossy paws rigid with venom."

11) HAIRDRESSER'S APPEAL SUCCEEDS: a barber who had been expelled from his union for practising his trade in factories was reinstated on the strength of his argument that it was better for factory workers to have their hair cut by professionals than by cut-price amateurs.

12) YOUTH THOUGHT HIS EARS PROTRUDED: an 18-year-old boy had become so self-conscious about his ears sticking out that at night he tried to plaster them back with adhesive tape, and was finally found dead in a gas-filled room.

Advertisements: 8 columns (half the page) of Public Appointments, Overseas Appointments, Business opportunities, Partnerships and Directorships, Situations, Domestic, Hotel and Club Staff Wanted, Drapery, Millinery, Tailoring, etc.

Pages 12 and 13

Solid advertisements: Announcements, Corporation Loans & Banks, Sales by Banks, Sales by Auction, Fashions, Contracts, Situations, Sales by Private Contract.

Also on page 13: Radio and TV programmes for that day.

Page 14

Fifteen news stories:

1) GERMANY MAY CONTRIBUTE £50M. TO KEEP BRITISH TROOPS, by "our own Correspondent", reported that the Anglo-German talks in Bonn about the cost of British troops in Western Germany had been broken off while the Germans had gone to another meeting in Paris; then filled two half-columns with hopeful speculation and informative gossip.

2) SYNTHETIC PETROL PLAN ABANDONED: a firm of manufacturing chemists which had hoped to produce 10,000 gallons of synthetic petrol a week had had to give up the scheme for lack of one ingredient.

* 3) MISS BETTERIDGE GOES TO POLICE: a 23-year-old girl who had been released from a mental hospital last July and had been missing from her foster-parents' home for a week, gave herself up at a police station. (An added fact which appeared in the *Guardian* but not in the *Mirror:* she returned to the mental hospital.)

4) SUBSIDENCE BILL: according to an M.P., if the cost of mining subsidence was put entirely on to the National Coal Board, miners would find it harder to get rises in future. In Staveley, where 500 post-war houses have had to be reinforced with steel "bandages" to prevent damage through subsidence, the National Coal Board will pay the bill.

5) FATHER ACCUSED OF WOUNDING: a few hours before she was to be married, Avril Johnson, 24, was taken to hospital with stab wounds. Her father, 71, a retired Jamaican sailor, was remanded in custody on a charge of wounding her.

6) LIBERALS CONDEMN BOMB TESTS: the Liberal party Council unanimously passed a resolution condemning atomic-bomb tests.

7) SUPREME CHAMPION AT CRUFT'S: top dog at Cruft's Show

at Olympia, London, over a record entry of 6,562, was a Keeshond, a Dutch barge dog.

* 8) CHILD'S 50-FT. FALL: (The *Guardian* added a fact not mentioned by the *Mirror*—"She was playing on an inside window sill when she leaned against the window which flew open.")

9) (No head) announced the death of M. Charles Faroux, 84, a leading French motor-racing journalist and man-about-the-world.

* 10) FIREMAN TRIED TO AVERT CRASH, by "our Special Correspondent" gave a much fuller account than appeared in the *Mirror* of the train wreck at Chapel-en-le-Frith. The most notable added fact: that John Axon, one of the two men killed, had stayed at the controls of his engine, in a desperate attempt to avert the crash.

11) EDUCATIONAL USES OF TELEVISION: at a weekend meeting in an adult educational college near Ripon the Warden of the college deplored the remark of the High Master of Manchester Grammar School, "that television would enter the school only over his dead body".

12) SANCTIONS OPPOSED: the Board of Deputies of British Jews appealed to the Government to oppose U.N. sanctions against Israel.

13) THREE ESCAPE FROM GUARDROOM: three privates of the York and Lancaster Regiment escaped yesterday from the guardroom at a Dover barracks, and are still at large.

* 14) P.C. "PEPPERED WITH SHOTS": a fuller account than appeared in the *Mirror*, and an additional fact—that the shots were pellets from a shotgun.

* 15) GIRL SHOT WHILE RIDING HORSE: to the facts in the *Mirror* report the *Guardian* added a statement from the girl's mother: "It was a .410 sporting gun and a number of the pellets penetrated her windcheater jacket and left marks on her back . . . two of the pellets are in her flesh, but the doctor says that they will work out."

Two photographs: of the train wreck at Chapel-en-le-Frith.

Conclusion of "PRAVDA'S" REPLY to M.Ps., carried over from p. 8.

Weather report and two weather charts.

A crossword puzzle.

Two advertisements: 1) A safe.
2) Births, Marriages and Deaths: an undertaker, and a crematorium.

STOP PRESS—empty.

BIBLIOGRAPHY

QUOTATIONS IN THIS book have been taken from the following sources:

Report of the Royal Commission on the Press—H.M. Stationery Office; *A Free and Responsible Press* (Report of the Commission on Freedom of the Press)—University of Chicago Press; *Lord Northcliffe*, by A. P. Ryan—William Collins Sons & Co.; *The Manchester Guardian, A Century of History*, by W. H. Mills—Chatto & Windus; *In Time of Trouble*, by Claud Cockburn—Rupert Hart-Davis; *The Press and the Public*, by George Blake—Faber & Faber; *C. P. Scott: The Making of the Manchester Guardian*—Frederick Muller; *A Hind Let Loose*, by C. E. Montague—Methuen & Co.; *Publish and Be Damned*, by Hugh Cudlipp—Andrew Dakers; *My Northcliffe Diary*, by Tom Clarke—Victor Gollancz; *C. P. Scott*, by J. L. Hammond—Bell Publishing Co.; *In the Meantime*, by Howard Spring—Constable & Co.; *History of the Times*—*The Times*; *Autobiography*, by Neville Cardus—William Collins Sons & Co.